START YOUR OWN
CANNABIS
BUSINESS

LEGAL DISCLAIMER

This book and its contents are intended for educational purposes only and should in no way be interpreted as medical, legal, or any other advice concerning the cultivation, sale, or any other use of marijuana, which although legal in some states and local jurisdictions throughout the United States, is at the time of publication of this book illegal under federal law, as well as in other states and local jurisdictions. The author and publisher do not advocate violating applicable law. Because of the variety of laws, regulations, and ordinances concerning marijuana and the fact that the advice and strategies contained herein may not be suitable for your situation, the author and publisher, make no expressed or implied warranties and assume no liability whatsoever, concerning the accuracy or reliability of the information contained herein, including warranties about the legality of, or likelihood of success in, conducting a cannabis business. The author and publisher recommend that anyone reading this book research applicable laws, and consult with appropriate licensed professionals and other experts, before taking any action in connection with, or based on, the contents of this book.

Additional titles in *Entrepreneur's Startup Series*

Start Your Own

Entrepreneur MAGAZINE'S

::: STARTUP

START YOUR OWN

CANNABIS

BUSINESS

YOUR STEP-BY-STEP GUIDE TO
THE MARIJUANA INDUSTRY

The Staff of Entrepreneur Media, Inc. & Javier Hasse

Entrepreneur
PRESS

Entrepreneur Press, Publisher
Cover Design: Andrew Welyczko
Production and Composition: Eliot House Productions

This publication is designed to provide accurate and authoritative information in regard to the subject matter covered. It is sold with the understanding that the publisher is not engaged in rendering legal, accounting or other professional services. If legal advice or other expert assistance is required, the services of a competent professional person should be sought.

Library of Congress Cataloging-in-Publication Data
    Names: Hasse, Javier, editor. | Entrepreneur Media, Inc., editor.
    Title: Start your own cannabis business: your step-by-step guide to the marijuana industry / by The
        Staff of Entrepreneur Media, Inc. and Javier Hasse.
    Description: Irvine : Entrepreneur Media, Inc., [2018]
    Identifiers: LCCN 2018001413| ISBN 978-1-59918-632-0 (alk. paper) | ISBN 1-59918-632-2 (alk. paper)
    Subjects: LCSH: Marijuana industry—United States—Management. | Marijuana—United States—
        Marketing. | New business enterprises—United States—Handbooks, manuals, etc.
    Classification: LCC HD9019.M382 U677 2018 | DDC 633.7/90688—dc23
    LC record available at https://lccn.loc.gov/2018001413

Printed in the United States of America

22 21 20 19 18   10 9 8 7 6 5 4 3 2 1

Contents

Foreword
by Jodie Emery
Cannabis Activist and Advocate

The cannabis industry appears to be one of the fastest-growing markets ever seen throughout North America, and it's expanding worldwide. With so much excitement and uncertainty about what the future holds, this is a valuable time to create opportunities of all kinds.

What was recently a mysterious underground subculture and industry has become increasingly mainstream with enormous public acceptance after decades of total prohibition. A wide range of people are now involved from the deeply-rooted pioneers, advocates, and providers of decades past to the newly-established pot businesses and investors—some of whom may have never touched a joint!

Cannabis is affecting every part of the economy, having an impact on farming, manufacturing, research, tourism, retail, entertainment, media, hospitality, and many other areas. Numerous sectors have been influenced by marijuana law reform; you don't even need to grow or sell the plant itself, because ancillary services are continuing to expand.

Why do you want to get involved in this exciting emerging cannabis industry? Where do you see yourself in this new legal landscape? That is the most important question to ask as you begin reading this book. The motivation behind your participation will have a big impact on your success over time.

With the legalization floodgates opening across North America and the world, mainstream money has been unleashed to help fuel the growth of cannabis companies. Venture capitalist and angel investors are looking for the best place to park funds and create profits. Countless individuals and businesses are competing with each other to establish brands and corporate models, hoping to capture a share of what's being touted as one of the biggest industries ever created.

In this new period of rapid growth, the "green rush" has ratcheted up competition. Increased choices and diversity leads to innovation, resulting in better products and services for consumers, but you have to be ready for the challenges of fast-paced change. Like any entrepreneur, you should get involved in something that matters to you, related to a vision or cause that you're passionate about.

So, what are you passionate about? What are your skills, and what expertise can you provide to help secure success? And most importantly: do you love cannabis? You should already have (or should begin cultivating) a love for the plant and what it represents if you want to be authentic and supported by consumers.

Cannabis isn't something new, so it's important to understand and respect the cannabis culture's deeply-rooted history. Aside from the massive and profoundly important topic of Drug War harms and reparations that are owed, especially to marginalized and radicalized people, there's also the history of the fledgling industry's struggle for acceptance.

Not too long ago, cannabis businesses were very rare. Finding bongs and pipes was problematic, and there were no public dispensaries beyond a very tiny number of West Coast jurisdictions serving medical marijuana patients. Thanks to decades of constant activism, advocacy, and political lobbying, laws and society have been slowly evolving to allow for the growth of many cannabis-related industries.

My husband, Marc Emery, was one of those early pioneers in the 1990s and the only business-focused activist in the movement. He promoted capitalism and enterprise to finance political advocacy, selling banned books and magazines like *High Times* and opening headshops to sell bongs, pipes, vaporizers, and other "illicit paraphernalia." He published *Cannabis Culture Magazine* and Pot TV and sold seeds over the counter and through the mail to the United States and worldwide. The seed money raised went right back to political law reform, and that's why so many supporters patronized his business—they knew his company was giving back to the community and cause.

There were—and still are—risks involved in the ever-changing cannabis industry. Millions of cannabis consumers, advocates, and entrepreneurs have been charged and jailed for cannabis-related crimes. In 2005, Marc was arrested by U.S. and Canadian police to face life in U.S. prison for funding legalization, as stated by the Drug Enforcement Administration. He ultimately pled guilty and served a five-year sentence, returning home to Canada in 2014.

Like some others, our long history of cannabis activism has been closely tied with our various businesses and that has earned enormous brand respect and loyalty. Our Cannabis Culture enterprise recently expanded to include dispensaries, which Marc and I were recently arrested and charged for. Long-established brands and businesses are rare, especially because the massive, deeply-entrenched, and long-established community has been forced to stay in the shadows of prohibition for so long.

But this new age of legalization is the perfect time for growth, innovation, and opportunities of all kinds. Now that marijuana is mainstream, it represents increasingly powerful economic influence. And all across North America, pioneers who have sacrificed to change pot laws, creating more access and liberty—and business opportunities—in the process, are hoping to find a place in the new legal industry. Hopefully this book will help them find inspiration and success!

We are all very fortunate to be witnessing a time of such significant legal, social, and political change. Cannabis isn't going away anytime soon . . . so dream big, focus on your passions, and always aim to be outstanding in your field!

Preface

Starting a business is always an uphill climb. From deciding on a business structure to finding a storefront location, the journey is long. And if you want to get started in the cannabis industry, that journey can take some unexpected turns. *Start Your Own Cannabis Business* will hopefully help you navigate those turns with a combination of useful information, tips, resources, and insightful stories about cannabis pioneers who have helped carve out the path for you.

Two of those entrepreneurs are Hunter Garth and Caleb Patton. The bearded Garth seems to be as chill as they come. After all, he works with marijuana.

But this was not always the case.

Returning home after serving with the United States Marine Corps in Afghanistan for four years was not easy. Readapting to civilian life was not easy. And, as you might imagine, overcoming the trauma of war was not easy—is it ever?

"During my life in deployment, I was hyper-exposed to trauma, but I really negated it all, telling myself that it was not that bad. I really took a tough-guy approach while I was in the Marine Corps," Garth reveals.

However, coming back home was a whole other issue. He could no longer live in denial. "My deployment had pretty extensive consequences. During my transitional period, I was not thinking right, I was not sleeping well, I wasn't handling things in an appropriate manner," he continues. He needed a change.

So Garth put his stuff in a U-Haul and, with 400 bucks in his pocket, moved from his home state of Florida to Colorado, and never looked back. Pretty much the opposite: he was now incentivizing his friends to do the same.

Recognizing a Light-Bulb Moment

Caleb Patton had served in Iraq and Afghanistan alongside Hunter Garth. Upon returning home, he had to undergo a calvary of his own. Suffering from excruciating physical and mental pain from an injury he got during a training accident in which seven of his fellow Marines were killed, Patton had turned to alcohol and pharmaceutical drugs. After a long quest, he found relief in cannabis. He never imagined weed would change his life—not only on a personal level but also on a financial one.

When Garth returned from Afghanistan, he found himself without a job, without a college education, and without any experience beyond being a Marine. He was 23 years old, and to a certain extent, it looked like the story of his life was over.

One day, he walked into a dispensary in Denver to get some cannabis, which helps him soothe and deal with posttraumatic stress more easily, and saw an armed guard. "His behavior, how he presented himself, and his general attitude were very off-putting," he describes.

He immediately thought that nobody wants to feel uncomfortable when buying weed. This was his a-ha moment: "I've got extensive knowledge about cannabis and a military background. I can do this better," he realized.

That same day, he decided to reach out to his friend Caleb to discuss his idea. This is how Iron Protection Group (IPG) came to be, formed by four former Marines without any outside funding or help from people with prior business experience.

The co-founders often say that IPG is not a security company that specializes in marijuana: it's a marijuana company that specializes in security. The concept is not hard to grasp: In an industry where each batch of product is worth tens of thousands of dollars and is not covered by insurance; where almost every transaction is made in cash; and where access to traditional banking is quite limited (we'll explain why later in this book), danger abounds. There are millions of dollars in product and actual cash sitting around at any given moment.

So what IPG does is make sure that everyone involved in producing, selling, and transporting the product and the money derived from it is safe—and feels that way.

"People are not necessarily afraid of guns but rather of the people using them," Garth contends when asked about the issue of IPG personnel carrying guns. "All our team served in the military and was in combat; we would literally go out and fight the Taliban. So we have extreme confidence around firearms and extreme training to use them correctly. However, we are also all very calm in our approach to threats and danger. We are quiet professionals. This means we know our jobs and our skills; we don't need to prove we are badass."

A Wide-Open Industry

As you'll find throughout this book, Garth's story is the embodiment of the cannabis industry's values—it shows that the industry is not just about growing and selling weed.

This is an industry that loves the Wall Street suit type as much as it loves the underdog and the guy or gal voted "least likely to succeed." There is space for anyone with good ideas and good intentions.

"We started IPG with four guys, and in about 60 days we already had 30 employees," Garth says. "We went from nothing to a multimillion-dollar business in literally two months, but none of us had business knowledge—we weren't even 25 years old. All we knew was there was a problem in the industry, and we could help fix it."

IPG went on to learn some hard—but valuable—business lessons along the way. Ultimately, Garth and Patton went on to ink an acquisition deal with General Cannabis, a $24 million, publicly traded company.

General Cannabis gave the IPG partners equity in the parent company while financing IPG and retaining the entirety of the team. This meant that IPG could now count on the support of a corporate structure (back office, legal, and financial backing) without having to actually sell out.

> **tip** ⓘ
>
> You can get the full version of IPG's story at http://entm.ag/u5j.

"This company was built by brothers helping brothers, and we intend to follow that path," Patton adds.

Effort + Vision = Success

This success story clearly shows how anyone—educated or not, connected or not, experienced or not—can make it in the cannabis industry. "I had made a million dollars, personally, by the time I turned 26," Garth discloses.

On the other hand, this story also provides numerous lessons about what's important when creating a business. Funding and expert advisory are central to the realization of a business idea; the fact that the guys at IPG got lucky does not mean anyone else will. In order to make it in the cannabis world, you'll need to plan ahead, raise money, and get good advice.

Having said that, know that you'll have to put a lot of effort into your business. "People think they will become rich overnight. But this is rarely the case. Cannabis today is a long-term play," Marvin Washington, Super Bowl champion turned cannabis investor and activist, points out.

"We could have been eaten alive in this process. Someone could have easily taken the company from our hands," Garth reflects. "I now understand the public space and the nuances of finance, but I didn't at the time. Education and mentorship were the most important takeaways from this experience."

"You need to be extremely confident on what you know, and get help with what you don't know," he advises.

So with these key principles in mind, let's get aboard the cannabis train. You are about to embark on what could be the adventure of the century in a movement that could redefine history forever.

Are you ready?

Let's go!

1

Introduction to Cannabis and the Marijuana Industry

The first thing anyone seeking to start a cannabis business needs to understand is the industry in which she will operate. While every industry is its own little universe, the marijuana industry is like no other.

This is an industry pierced by controversy, by social and racial issues, and by strong economic interests. It impacts (almost always positively) health care, drug abuse and overdose figures, the number of opioid prescriptions, taxation, public finances, agriculture, the jobs market, real estate, criminal justice, gender inequality, the correctional system, the environment, and the stock market. You name it, and weed legalization will probably have some kind of effect on it.

So let's take a closer look at the world of weed and what it holds for you and your future as a cannabis entrepreneur.

Cannabis by the Numbers

An interesting way to frame the significance of the cannabis industry is to look at the numbers for legal cannabis sales in the U.S. and compare them to the additional economic impact of these businesses, which includes things like the wages paid to their employees, state and local taxes paid by the businesses, and real estate and construction activity generated by the launch of a new cannabis business. Check out Figure 1–1.

It's no wonder that cannabis impacts the economy when you consider how the general population feels about it. "I think that one of the things that really attracts a lot of people to the cannabis industry is that they feel like they are making a positive difference in the

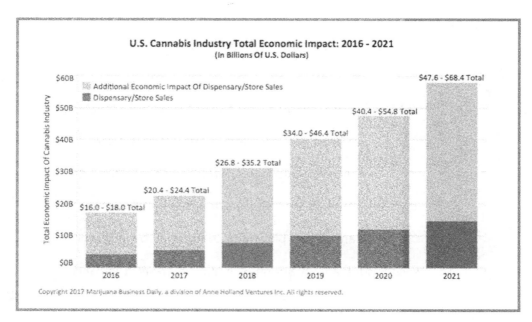

FIGURE 1–1: **U.S. Cannabis Industry Economic Impact**
Source: Marijuana Business Daily's "Marijuana Business Factbook 2017."

FIGURE 1–2: **U.S. Marijuana Enthusiasm Index**
Source: AZMarijuana.com. Find it at https://azmarijuana.com/dans-stash/map-u-s-marijuana-enthusiasm-index/.

world," adds Diane Stratford Czarkowski, co-founder of marijuana consulting firm Canna Advisors.

Check out the level of enthusiasm for cannabis in each U.S. state in Figure 1–2.

This enthusiasm didn't happen overnight, though. Cannabis has a long history both culturally and as a business. So before moving on, we'll share a bird's-eye view of the evolution of cannabis use and legislation in the U.S.

How We Got Here: A Bit of History

Marijuana use can be traced back more than 4,500 years with early adoption in China, Siberia, India, and Nepal, among other places. However, its regulated use in the U.S. is what interests us the most. So let's fast-forward to the turn of the 20th century.

Regulations that mentioned hemp-based drugs were first introduced in the U.S. in 1885 and 1889. In 1906, the U.S. Congress passed the Pure Food and Drug Act, which created labeling requirements for certain drugs, including cannabis, but enforcement was not widespread.

Cannabis preparations were still easy to get until the 1930s with popular medications like "One Night Cough Syrup" and "Piso's Cure" containing cannabis. Only in the fourth decade of the century did marijuana prohibition really kick in. It all started with the Uniform Narcotic Drug Act of 1932 and continued with the Marihuana Tax Act of 1937, which imposed "an occupational excise tax upon certain dealers in marijuana (…) a transfer tax upon certain dealings in marijuana," and safeguarded "the revenue there from by registry and recording." While the law did not make cannabis illegal, it was used by law enforcement to arrest dealers and users, arguing they were not paying these taxes.

The real change, nonetheless, came with the infamous 1936 propaganda film *Reefer Madness* (see Figures 1–3 below and 1–4 on page 5 for some now-funny ads railing against marijuana) and the 1938 Federal Food, Drug, and Cosmetic Act, which created a framework for the U.S. Food and Drug Administration (FDA) to regulate cannabis.

FIGURE 1–3: **Anti-Cannabis Propaganda from the 1930s**
Public domain.

FIGURE 1–4: **Anti-Cannabis Propaganda from the 1930s**
Public domain.

But probably the most relevant milestones in this trajectory to illegality were the 1952 Boggs Act and the Narcotic Control Act of 1956, which established mandatory sentencing for marijuana-related crimes and made punishment for such offenses much more significant.

The "War on Drugs" and What It Means Today

Nowadays, most of these regulations are no longer valid. The current, applicable law derives from the 1970 Controlled Substances Act (CSA), which repealed the Marihuana Tax Act, creating a new federal policy that regulated the manufacturing, importation, possession, use, and distribution of certain substances. The CSA created five categories for these substances based on their accepted medical uses, safety profiles, and potential for abuse.

Under the new CSA, cannabis was categorized as a Schedule I drug. These are "drugs with no currently accepted medical use and a high potential for abuse," the DEA argues, putting cannabis in the same category as heroin, lysergic acid diethylamide (LSD), and 3,4-methylenedioxymethamphetamine (ecstasy). They even deemed it less useful than cocaine, methamphetamine and crystal meth, and fentanyl.

As reference, Table 1–1 contains a few examples of drugs in each one of the DEA's five categories or schedules, determined by the agency's conception of their "acceptable medical use" and their dependency or abuse potential.

The final piece of legislation relevant to this framework is the 1986 Anti-Drug Abuse Act, signed by President Ronald Reagan, which established the much-discussed mandatory minimum prison sentences and the infamous "three-strikes" policy. This act allowed Reagan's successor in the White House, George H.W. Bush, to commence the so-called "war on drugs" in 1989.

The aforementioned "tough on crime" laws forced judges to sentence people for petty offenses, obliging them to hand out unreasonably long prison sentences for simple drug possession and very small sales even among medical users.

"The war on drugs is actually a war on people," co-owner of online magazine *Cannabis Culture* and famed cannabis activist Jodie Emery concludes. "It is a war that is being used to hurt people and violate their civil liberties. The number of gross human rights abuses and civil rights violations that go on every day under the name of the war on cannabis or the war on drugs (justified by the argument that cannabis is dangerous,

Schedule I	Schedule II	Schedule III	Schedule IV	Schedule V
Heroin	Vicodin	Ketamine	Xanax	Robitussin AC
Lysergic acid diethylamide (LSD)	Cocaine	Anabolic steroids (Bodybuilding drugs)	Valium	Lomotil
3,4-methylenedioxy-methamphetamine (ecstasy)	Methamphetamine	Testosterone	Ambien	Motofen
Methaqualone (Quaaludes)	Oxycodone (OxyContin)	Aspirin with codeine	Tramadol	Lyrica
Peyote	Fentanyl	Buprenorphine	Ativan	Parepectolin
Marijuana (cannabis)	Adderall	Benzphetamine	Soma	

TABLE 1–1: **Examples of Drugs in Each of DEA's Five Categories or Schedules**
Source: DEA Drug Scheduling. Find it at https://www.dea.gov/druginfo/ds.shtml.

which is not true) is exasperating. In the end, the law hurt much more people than cannabis ever will."

In 2014, the U.S. witnessed more than 1.5 million drug-related arrests. Eighty percent of them were for simple possession and almost half for marijuana-related offenses, Emery points out. A 2016 study from Human Rights Watch showed that nearly 600,000 people are arrested for possession of cannabis in the U.S. every year. That means that more than one person is arrested every minute of the year for holding weed; it also means that more people are arrested for cannabis crimes than for all violent offenses combined. Notably, the system continues to criminalize minorities with these low-level cannabis busts. Although black and white people use cannabis at roughly comparable rates, black people were four times as likely to be arrested for possessing it.

"People of color, minorities, all sorts of marginalized groups, are disproportionately targeted, criminalized, even in a legal framework," Emery points out.

So what does this mean for you, the prospective cannabis business owner? It means that the business you are entering has had a long history of legal and cultural challenges. Because of that, the industry is constantly adapting to the laws and regulations that govern it—and you.

> **tip**
>
> Keep up-to-date on all local, state, and federal laws pertaining to cannabis use so your business can adapt quickly.

THC and CBD

Before getting into the current legal status of cannabis across the U.S., we need to understand the basics of the cannabis plant and its components as very diverse business opportunities can derive from each one.

Scientists are still researching and learning about the cannabis plant and its genetic profile. While we are discovering new things about marijuana, we have known for many years now that the two main chemical compounds in weed are delta-9-tetrahydrocannabinol (THC) and cannabidiol (CBD).

THC and CBD are part of a family of active chemical ingredients that cannabis (and other) plants produce, called cannabinoids. While there are many interesting facts about these compounds, all you really need to know for the time being is the difference between THC, THCa, and CBD.

THCa is a non-psychoactive chemical present in cannabis plants, which, when dried, loses its "a" (or acid) component, creating THC, the so-called psychoactive ingredient in weed. Consequently, THC is often responsible for getting cannabis users "high" or "stoned." If you're thinking about starting a business aimed at recreational cannabis users, this is the compound that should interest you the most.

Due to THC's psychoactivity, most countries are still cautious about allowing its use. However, THC is believed to have other properties beyond the recreational experience, like stimulating the appetite, suppressing nausea, treating inflammation and insomnia, and so on.

Ram Mukunda, CEO of cannabis pharmaceutical company IGC, agrees. "Further, there is scientific evidence that low doses of THC that are too small to cause inebriation can help Alzheimer's patients alleviate many of their adverse symptoms," he says. "This is an unexplored pathway as most of the research focuses on higher dosage of THC that causes patients to get high."

CBD, on the other hand, is believed to have no psychoactive effects and can even be extracted from industrial hemp and hops plants. In fact, it is often said that CBD actually reduces the psychoactive sensation generated by THC. As such, it is frequently used to treat children and adults suffering from epilepsy and other grave ailments and brain disorders. So if you're looking at the medical or wellness side of cannabis, pay close attention to CBD and high-CBD cannabis strains and products.

Figure 1–5 on page 9 shows a chart taken from Leafly.com. On the left side you'll find THC, which "directly stimulates the CB1 receptor. This interaction underlies the major psychoactive effects of cannabis consumption," the accompanying article explains.

On the right side of the image is CBD, which "reduces, or 'antagonizes,' THC's ability to stimulate CB1 receptors. This can decrease some of THC's effects, especially negative effects like anxiety and short-term memory impairment," the author adds.

"Naturally occurring compounds in cannabis occur in different proportions and often have opposite effects. This is the case of THC and CBD for psychosis risk, for example," Dr. Godfrey Pearlson, a professor at Yale University's School of Medicine and director of the Olin Neuropsychiatry Research Center, comments.

Given its lack of psychoactivity, the use of CBD products like oils and other extracts is allowed in many countries, sometimes even without a medical prescription. Some countries that have at least depenalized the use of CBD products are Argentina, Austria, Belgium, Belize, Brazil, Bulgaria, Canada, Chile, China, Colombia, Costa Rica, Croatia, Cyprus, Czech Republic, Denmark, Estonia, Finland, France, Georgia, Germany, Greece, Guam, Guatemala, Hungary, Iceland, India, Ireland, Italy, Latvia, Lithuania, Luxembourg, the Netherlands, Netherlands Antilles, Northern Ireland, Norway, Paraguay, Peru, Poland, Portugal, Puerto Rico, Romania, Russia, Slovenia, South Africa, Sweden, Switzerland, the U.S., Uruguay, and the U.S. Virgin Islands.

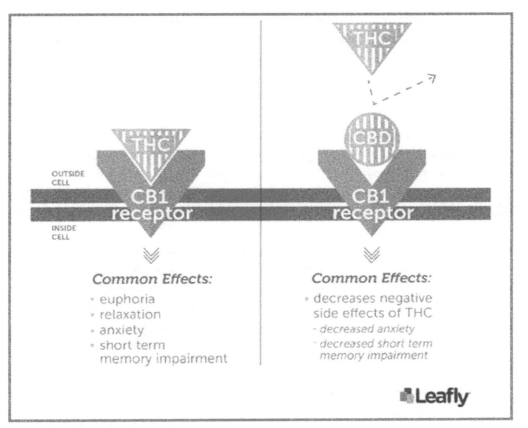

FIGURE 1–5: **THC vs. CBD**
Source: Amy Phung/Leafly. Find it at www.leafly.com/news/science-tech/cbd-vs-thc-cbd-not-intoxicating.

In addition, the World Anti-Doping Agency, which is responsible for drug testing among Olympic athletes and tends to set the criteria for anti-doping in most sports across the globe, removed CBD from its list of banned substances in 2017. Other natural and synthetic cannabinoids like THC remain prohibited, but as of 2018, athletes around the globe will be allowed to use CBD—assuming laws in their countries permit it.

The Current Legal Landscape

All this history lays the groundwork for what matters most to you as a cannabis entrepreneur— the current legal landscape. A handful of legal cases, including *Printz v. United States* (1997), *Crosby v. National Foreign Trade Council* (2000), and *Gonzales v. Raich* (2005), set the precedent for the legislation that, to a certain extent, regulates legal cannabis today. As a potential business owner, you need to remember that the largest challenges related to starting and operating a cannabis business stem from legal compliance. In other words, there is no way around this section: if you own a marijuana business, you need to know everything about the laws that apply and the history behind them. Think of it as your crash course in legalization.

Back to business: the first major milestone in legalization was the Ogden Memo of October 19, 2009, conceived as a guide for U.S. Attorneys on "the exercise of investigative and prosecutorial discretion." The intention was to steer the use of investigative and prosecutorial resources away from "individuals whose actions are in clear and unambiguous compliance with existing state laws providing for the medical use of marijuana" and toward "significant traffickers of illegal drugs, including marijuana, and the disruption of illegal drug manufacturing and trafficking networks."

A couple of years later, in 2011, Deputy Attorney General James M. Cole issued a memorandum of his own: the first Cole Memo. The memo was intended to provide legal protection for caregivers ("individuals providing care to individuals with cancer or other serious illnesses, not commercial operations cultivating, selling, or distributing marijuana") and reiterated the importance of prosecuting drug traffickers (rather than state-legal producers and retailers) established in the Ogden Memo, although it did not protect legal cultivators from federal prosecution.

warning ⚠

Laws may have changed yet again since this book was written. Be sure to check with your local and state governing bodies for the most up-to-date legalization information.

Finally, there's the so-called Cole Memo 2.0 of 2013, which was applicable until Attorney General Jeff Sessions controversially rescinded it in 2018. This memo exhorted federal authorities to stay out of states' issues, letting local law enforcement agencies and regulators decide the fate of their legal cannabis businesses, incentivizing a "hands-off" approach.

A memo from the Office of the Attorney General, Jeff Sessions, dated January 4, 2018, rescinds the Obama-era policies (most notably the Cole memo) that paved the way for country-wide legalization. As of this writing, AG Sessions has returned the power to decide how to enforce federal cannabis laws to federal law enforcement agencies and U.S. attorneys around the country. But for the time being, it seems that most U.S. attorneys in states with legal marijuana are not willing to waste their time and government resources prosecuting legal cannabis businesses and consumers.

"The other important piece of legislation is the Rohrabacher-Farr amendment or Rohrabacher-Blumenauer amendment, which doesn't allow any money to be spent prosecuting state-legal medical marijuana businesses—although it ends up applying to recreational business as well," Bradley Blommer, a litigation and real estate attorney with Green Light Law Group, comments.

With the help of international law expert Zameer Qureshi, we have come up with a list of some additional literature that you can check out if you're interested in learning more about the history of cannabis, its prohibition, and its relegalization around the world:

▶ Abel, Ernest L. *Marihuana: The First Twelve Thousand Years*. Springer, 1980.

▶ Barcott, Bruce. *Weed the People: The Future of Legal Marijuana in America*. Time Books, 2015.

▶ Blaszczak-Boxe, Agata. "Marijuana's History: How One Plant Spread Through the World." *Live Science* (October 17, 2014). www.livescience.com/48337-marijuana-history-how-cannabis-travelled-world.html

▶ Clarke, Robert C. and Mark D. Merlin. *Cannabis: Evolution and Ethnobotany*. University of California Press, 2016.

▶ Drug Policy Alliance. *A Brief History of the Drug War*. www.drugpolicy.org/issues/brief-history-drug-war.

▶ Holland, Julie, ed. *The Pot Book: A Complete Guide to Cannabis*. Park Street Press, 2010.

▶ Jones, Nick. *Spliffs: A Celebration of Cannabis Culture*. Chrysalis Impact, 2003.

▶ Kalant, Harold. "Medicinal Use of Cannabis: History and Current Status." *Pain Research and Management* 6, no. 2 (Summer 2001): 80–94.

▶ Mikuriya, T. H. "Marijuana in Medicine: Past, Present and Future." *California Medicine* 110, no. 1 (January 1969): 34.

▶ NORML. *Marijuana Law Reform Timeline*. http://norml.org/shop/item/marijuana-law-reform-timeline.

▶ PBS. *Busted—America's War on Marijuana*. www.pbs.org/wgbh/pages/frontline/shows/dope/etc/cron.html.

▶ Russo, E. B. "History of Cannabis and Its Preparations in Saga, Science, and Sobriquet." *Chemistry & Biodiversity* 4, no. 8 (August 2007): 1614–1648.

▶ Walton, R. P. *Marihuana, America's New Drug Problem: A Sociologic Question with Its Basic Explanation Dependent on Biologic and Medical Principles*. JB Lippincott Company, 1938.

Take into account that the landscape of the cannabis business evolves constantly and rapidly, so things may change at any given moment. Having said this, let's take a look at the steadier variables—those that are not likely to transform overnight.

▶ A G20 President Weighs In

Vicente Fox Quesada is the former president of Mexico and a Harvard Business School alum. In recent years, he's become a vocal advocate of cannabis legalization, presenting his arguments in numerous public events across the U.S. So we decided to ask him to share a message for American cannabis entrepreneurs.

In his view, the United States is currently going through a migration process, from illegality to legality, from prohibition to regulation. "This process starts with education, with a formation of public opinion," he says. "But this takes time.

"We need citizens, families, and communities to become comfortable with the idea that everything will work better with [cannabis] legalization and regulation. For this to happen, it's crucial that people come to terms with the fact that cannabis is not all bad, that there's a good side to it, and that we need to take advantage of its medical and other benefits.

"Once this process of transformation of public opinion gets going and reaches majority (or close to majority) levels, the political guild will intervene and proceed to legalize cannabis, to convert this into a regulated arena that responds to the population's real needs," he continues.

"We've seen this kind of policy succeed in numerous U.S. states as well as across the globe in places like the Netherlands, Portugal, and Uruguay," Mr. Fox points out. "So why not take it to a federal level everywhere?"

"Only when we proceed to legalize we will see this business taken away from traffickers' and cartels' hands and put in the hands of entrepreneurs, allowing for planning, regulation, a market, strategy . . . all the tools available in the [legal] business world," he adds. "This is the only way to really promote economic growth in the cannabis sector, taking it from the underground to the mainstream—to the business world."

"Why benefit vicious drug cartels when hard-working Americans could be the ones reaping the economic benefits of cannabis production and trade?" he asks. "Legalization is the way to stop violence and turn it into economic prosperity."

Understanding Cannabis Legalization in the U.S.

Cannabis legalization is sweeping through the world from South America to Oceania and from Africa to Western Europe—and the U.S. is no exception. Even though at the time of

FIGURE 1–6: **Legalization in the U.S.**
Source: NORML.

this writing marijuana remains a DEA Schedule I, federally illegal substance, eight states (Alaska, California, Colorado, Maine, Massachusetts, Nevada, Oregon, and Washington) and the District of Columbia have laws in place to allow adults to use weed recreationally. In addition, 22 more states permit the use of marijuana for medicinal purposes, while 16 others have CBD-specific laws, which don't allow pot per se, but tolerat some non-psychoactive cannabis derivatives.

Figure 1–6 shows a (slightly edited) screenshot from an interactive map that can be found at http://norml.org/laws.

Even though the legal status of cannabis may have changed since its publication (see the timeline in Figure 1–7 on page 14) on a state or even federal level, it's important to comprehend the difference between the diverse levels of legality of cannabis. To put it simply, the U.S. has:

▶ Places where cannabis remains illegal. Period.

Timeline of State Marijuana Legalization Laws

1996	1997	1998	1999	2000	2001	2002	2003	2004	2005	2006
California		Alaska	Maine	Colorado				Montana	Rhode Island	
		Oregon		Hawaii				Vermont		
		Washington		Nevada						

2007	2008	2009	2010	2011	2012	2013	2014	2015	2016	2017
New Mexico			Arizona	Delaware	Illinois		Maryland		West Virginia	
	Michigan		New Jersey		New Hampshire		Minnesota		Arkansas	
			Washington, DC		Connecticut		New York		Florida	
					Massachusetts		Alaska		North Dakota	
					Colorado		Oregon		Ohio	
					Washington		Washington, DC		Pennsylvania	
									California	
									Maine	
									Massachusetts	
									Nevada	

Recreational (8 states & DC)   Medical (29 states & DC)

FIGURE 1–7: **Timeline of State Marijuana Legalization Laws**
Source: Civilized.life. Find it at https://www.civilized.life/articles/evolution-america-marijuana-laws-charts/.

► Places where *some* derivatives of the cannabis or hemp plant are legal under medical prescription. These places tend to allow the use of CBD-based therapeutics and other non-psychoactive cannabinoid-based products.

► Places where the cannabis plant and its derivatives are legal under medical prescription.

► Places where any adult can use marijuana for recreational purposes under certain conditions (which vary from location to location).

While this simple categorization might help you get started, it's fundamental to know that there are many levels of regulation within each market. Any business in the industry is subject not only to federal and state rules and guidelines, but also to municipal and local protocols, procedures, and directives.

You should get guidance from a professional team that's up to date with all these different regulatory levels as well as consider using some kind of software to keep track of the ever-evolving laws (if it's available in your state). A few compliance software providers include CannaRegs, which tracks and aggregates the diverse laws, regulations, and taxes that apply to any cannabis business at the municipal, state, and federal levels; iComply Cannabis; MJ Freeway Business Solutions; WebJoint; Complia; and Simplifya. With these platforms, users can easily find all the rules that apply to their business and set up alerts to remain updated on any changes.

For practical purposes, this book will focus on starting businesses in states with full-blown medical marijuana programs and adult use states as these encompass most of the legal market and offer the lowest barriers to entry. While we'll be looking into the U.S. opportunity in particular, most of our suggestions should apply to numerous other overseas markets like Israel, Germany, Canada, Uruguay, Switzerland, and Australia, just to name a few.

While it might sound somewhat counterintuitive, government regulation creates opportunity. "Actually, the greatest wealth creation has usually come out of regulated industries," famed cannabis investor Micah Tapman, who likes to think of himself as an "oddly skeptical yet optimistic venture capitalist," comments. "If you take the time to understand this regulated industry, you take the time to solve its complexities, then you'll be one of the only people operating there. So, quite frankly, you'll have more room to operate."

To supplement the tilt of U.S. states with legalized recreational marijuana, Table 1–2 shows a list of U.S. states that only have legalized medical marijuana—as of December 2016:

U.S. States with Legalized Medical Marijuana	
Arizona	Arkansas
Connecticut	Delaware
Florida	Hawaii
Illinois	Louisiana
Maryland	Michigan
Minnesota	Montana
New Hampshire	New Jersey
New Mexico	New York
North Dakota	Ohio
Pennsylvania	Rhode Island
Vermont	West Virginia

TABLE 1–2: **U.S. States with Legalized Medical Marijuana**
Source: DEA Drug Scheduling. Find it at www.dea.gov/druginfo/ds.shtml.

The Cannabis Market

Another important thing to know before getting into the marijuana industry is what the current market looks like. There are many different estimates for cannabis sales. Since most of the top analytics firms in the space collaborated in New Frontier Data's "The Cannabis Industry Annual Report: 2017 Legal Marijuana Outlook," you can use their figures as reference.

As per New Frontier Data's estimates, legal cannabis sales in North America reached about $6.6 billion in 2016; recreational marijuana sales accounted for roughly 29 percent, while the remaining 71 percent went to medical marijuana. Although significant, the $6.6 billion still represents less than 12 percent of the total $56 billion Arcview Market Research estimates North Americans spent on weed last year.

"Legalization is supposed to accomplish three goals: to stop criminalizing people for pot (when it's nonviolent, peaceful people); to stop criminalizing the existing industry, which is worth billions and already out there; and to stop spending law enforcement money on marijuana law enforcement," *Cannabis Culture's* Jodie Emery argues.

Scott Greiper is the president of Viridian Capital Advisors, an investment bank and advisory practice in the legal cannabis industry. "One of the more unique dynamics of the cannabis industry is that it is a very large cottage industry—by Bloomberg measures, $40 billion to $50 billion in annual cannabis consumption in the U.S.," he points out, predicting a migration toward industrial-scale providers run by executives with proven track records in other industries over the next few years.

While estimates might provide a clear picture of what to expect in terms of the market size and potential, understanding how many Americans live in states with legalized marijuana (see Figure 1–8) can help you make some back-of-the-envelope calculations of your own.

Legal sales are currently surging at a compound annual growth rate of 16 percent; New Frontier expects them to surpass $24 billion by 2025. Over the longer term and under a federally legal regime, Greiper has argued that the U.S. marijuana market (including ancillary businesses) could exceed $100 billion in value.

Adding to the point about growth, Arcview Market Research's editor in chief Tom Adams says, "I've covered a long series of entrepreneur-started, rapidly growing industries, from home video and cable television to the internet, and I have seen only one other industry that has the growth prospects that cannabis has, and that was the broadband internet industry."

By way of comparison, Adams points out that the broadband Internet industry reached $5 billion in revenue and then continued to grow at a more-than-30 percent compound annual growth rate over the following five years. Similarly, Arcview expects the North

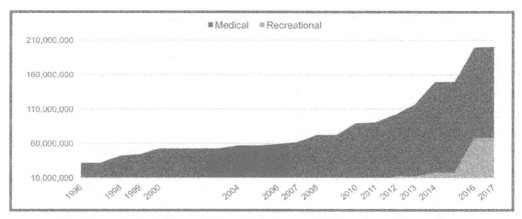

FIGURE 1–8: **Number of Americans Living in States with Legalized Marijuana**
Source: Civilized.life. Find it at www.civilized.life/articles/evolution-america-marijuana-laws-charts/.

American cannabis industry to grow at a 27 percent CAGR over the next five years. Figure 1–9 illustrates one of these growth projections.

"The industry is at about 5 percent of what it will be someday," concurs Tyler Stratford, director of client operations for cannabis consulting firm Canna Advisors. "Even if the path

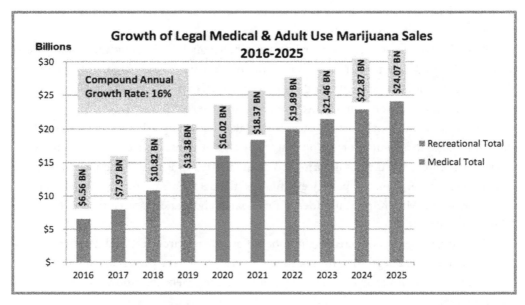

FIGURE 1–9: **Growth of Legal Medical and Adult Use Marijuana Sales**
Source: New Frontier Data.

forward is not straight, we are certainly on a path forward. The tide has changed, and there is no turning it back now."

No matter which numbers you look at, one thing is clear: a booming market with a pre-existing demand like the marijuana market creates an unprecedented opportunity for business ventures of all sizes and natures. And, as can be seen in Figure 1–9 on page 17, it's not just medical marijuana that will be extremely profitable. Recreational cannabis also holds great promise. As Tom Adams, who also serves as BDS Analytics' managing director and principal analyst, puts it, "Cannabis is the next big thing in home entertainment."

Furthermore, according to Marijuana Business Daily's "Marijuana Business Factbook 2017," in 2016, roughly 70 percent of wholesale cultivators, retailers, and infused-product manufacturers declared they had hit or surpassed their break-even point within a year.

While the 2017 survey revealed that this number had tumbled to 55 percent, the figures were still impressive, given that most other industries have a two- to three-year break-even period.

While researching for his own book on cannabis and the capital markets, Leslie Bocskor, investment banker and president of cannabis advisory firm Electrum Partners, looked into many other industries' average break-even times and has not found any other where "that many businesses reach break-even within a year. I don't think there is any historical reference that comes close."

"This fact acquires even more relevance when you look at how many businesses typically fail and do not reach break-even within three years. It really highlights how much economic power is being shifted into this industry, which then is going to translate, in many ways, into dramatic changes in how we live," Bocskor asserts.

On the flip side, marijuana businesses operate in a legal grey area. This means they often lack access to a lot of information that traditional businesses have. "This new industry is very fragmented, and there is not a lot of data out there. Things are changing, but we need human intelligence, human experience to filter all the data that's becoming available and to make sense of it," Matt Karnes, founder of financial analysis and research firm GreenWave Advisors points out.

There are, however, an increasing number of private research and analytics firms being founded, and they are beginning to create the knowledge necessary to establish the industry. Here is a list of the top analytics firms (with links to their websites) and what kind of data each one tracks:

▶   The Arcview Group generates in-depth market research: https://arcviewgroup.com

- ▶ Baker Technologies focuses mostly on point-of-sales and customer data: www.trybaker.com
- ▶ BDS Analytics also offers point-of-sales data, in addition to consumer research and industry intelligence: www.bdsanalytics.com
- ▶ Cannabis Benchmarks has one of the most complete data sets on the wholesale market: www.cannabisbenchmarks.com
- ▶ Consumer Research Around Cannabis creates cross-referenced local consumer preferences data: www.consumerresearcharoundcannabis.com
- ▶ Eaze shares sales data and consumer preferences information: www.eaze.com
- ▶ GreenWave Advisors releases reports on the state of the industry, lab testing, retail sales, and the coexistence of legalized medical and recreational use marijuana markets: www.greenwaveadvisors.com
- ▶ Headset focuses on market data, business intelligence, and retailer-direct data: http://headset.io
- ▶ Marijuana Business Daily publishes reports on financial benchmarks and business facts, as well as a licenses directory: https://mjbizdaily.com
- ▶ New Frontier Data dives deep into the state of legal cannabis markets across the globe, and in numerous U.S. states; sales projections; diversity reports; investor studies; tax collection and potential estimates; and industrywide trends: https://newfrontierdata.com
- ▶ Viridian Capital Advisors tracks stock performance, capital raises, and M&A activity in the public and private sectors: www.viridianca.com

▶ Cultivating Cannabis Employment

According to Marijuana Business Daily's "Marijuana Business Factbook 2017," there were a total of 20,000 to 28,000 cannabis businesses in the U.S. that year. Retailers represented the largest category dealing directly with the product with 3,300 to 4,300 businesses, followed by wholesale cultivators (2,500 to 3,500), and infused-products manufacturers (1,600 to 2,000). Ancillary services, products, and technology companies accounted for the remaining 13,000 to 18,000 businesses in the space.

These businesses employed an estimated 165,000 to 230,000 people nationwide with 80,000 to 110,000 of these employees actually working directly with marijuana.

In conclusion, Max Simon, founder and CEO of Green Flower Media, the largest online cannabis education platform, says: "While the cannabis industry is exploding with opportunity, possibility, and growth, it's also a very, very difficult business landscape to operate in. So what that means is that people should be prepared to be resilient. This is an industry that will require more work, more time, more patience, more risk than just about anything else."

What this means for you, the entrepreneur, is that you will need to brace yourself for a few years of hard work—and a lot of personal satisfaction, too. It all starts with research, so before you dive into starting your business, you should familiarize yourself with some of the most important industry background information you need to know (beyond the legal info). One of the best topics to start with is high on everyone's radar these days: medical marijuana.

Medical Marijuana

Cannabis has been proven to have medicinal properties—this is no longer anecdotal. Understanding that marijuana is actual medicine is fundamental to anyone starting a business around medical cannabis.

"Because cannabis is a Schedule I substance, there has been a dearth of research, of properly controlled, double-blind, placebo-controlled, crossover trials of cannabis as a medication. So a lot of the information we really need has not been produced because the government has stood in the way of proper clinical trials," Dr. Godfrey Pearlson explains, implicitly suggesting another line of business: clinical trials and medical research.

However, there are an increasing number of peer-reviewed scientific studies showing the diverse medical properties of this plant and its components—see bullet list below. "We now know that cannabis cannot only help greatly ill people, but [that] it also has wellness benefits for many other people," Arcview's Tom Adams comments, paving the way for wellness-related (non-clinical) businesses as well.

"The medical benefits of marijuana have been studied; they are no longer a myth. What *is* a myth is the assumption that by smoking marijuana you will get all the benefits of cannabis," says Aras Azadian, CEO of Avicanna, a Canadian cannabinoid therapeutics company, which was the first cannabis-related company to be admitted into Johnson & Johnson Innovation, JLABS @ Toronto—proving that cannabis businesses can also be mainstream ones.

Understanding marijuana legalization and the medical benefits of cannabis becomes particularly important in the context of the opioid crisis that is hitting America so hard,

Brendan Hill argues. Hill is the drummer for rock band Blues Traveler and owner of a cannabis dispensary in Washington state. "There are numerous reports from states with legalized marijuana that show that opioid use and abuse has come down and death rates have come down," he says.

"There is reasonable evidence that, where states have legalized medical marijuana for a variety of purposes, opioid prescription and death rates actually do fall significantly," Dr. Pearlson confirms. So if you happen to live in a state where opioids are a prevailing problem, you can certainly find a way to help by starting a cannabis business.

> **warning** ⚠
>
> You should take into account that, while cannabis is believed to not generate addiction, it can spawn dependence. Also notice that long-term effects have not been fully studied yet.

Beyond treating addiction, cannabis is used for many other disorders. "If you follow the science, you will come to the logical conclusion that the medicinal benefits of cannabis are real. Cannabis has helped out with some indications and illnesses that Western medicine has usually treated with opiates and other pharmaceuticals that are detrimental to people's health," Super Bowl champion turned cannabis advocate Marvin Washington says.

"To me, cannabis is not about getting high; it's about getting patients to feel better. If we can show that people are medicating responsibly and doing it to feel well, we'll be able to change the narrative around the plant," he adds. However, changing the narrative also implies getting people to understand that, while cannabis can treat a lot of conditions, it's not the cure-all that some people like to present it as. So as vast as the opportunities in this space might be, not every idea can translate into a viable company.

Instead of discussing the literature and science behind the use of cannabis to treat certain ailments in depth, as it is such a comprehensive topic, we've decided to share a list of the main qualifying medical conditions in the U.S.—meaning the disorders that at least *one* state considers justify the prescription of medical marijuana to a patient:

- ▶ Acquired immunodeficiency syndrome (AIDS)
- ▶ ADHD
- ▶ Alzheimer's disease
- ▶ Amyotrophic lateral sclerosis (ALS) or Lou Gehrig's disease
- ▶ Anorexia
- ▶ Arthritis
- ▶ Autism
- ▶ Cachexia, or wasting syndrome

- Cancer
- Cerebral palsy
- Chronic pain
- Crohn's disease
- Cystic fibrosis
- Decompensated cirrhosis
- Depression
- Dravet syndrome
- Dystonia
- Epilepsy and seizures
- Fibromyalgia
- Fibrous dysplasia
- Glaucoma
- Hepatitis C
- Human immunodeficiency virus (HIV)
- Huntington's disease
- Hydrocephalus
- Hydromyelia
- Inclusion body myositis
- Inflammatory bowel disease (IBD)
- Insomnia
- Interstitial cystitis
- Lennox-Gastaut syndrome
- Lupus
- Migraines (intractable)
- Multiple sclerosis (MS)
- Muscular dystrophy
- Myoclonus
- Nail-patella syndrome
- Neurofibromatosis
- Neuropathies
- Parkinson's disease
- Post-concussion syndrome
- Post-laminectomy syndrome with chronic radiculopathy
- Post-traumatic stress disorder (PTSD)
- Reflex sympathetic dystrophy

tip

For an up-to-date, state-by-state list of qualifying conditions, check out www.leafly.com/news/health/qualifying-conditions-for-medical-marijuana-by-state.

- ▶ Residual limb pain
- ▶ Rheumatoid arthritis (RA)
- ▶ Severe nausea
- ▶ Severe psoriasis and psoriatic arthritis
- ▶ Sickle cell disease
- ▶ Spasmodic torticollis (cervical dystonia)
- ▶ Spasticity
- ▶ Spastic quadriplegia
- ▶ Spinal cord injury or disease
- ▶ Spinocerebellar ataxia
- ▶ Syringomyelia
- ▶ Tarlov cysts
- ▶ Terminal illness (with short life expectancy)
- ▶ Tourette syndrome
- ▶ Traumatic brain injury (TBI)
- ▶ Trigeminal neuralgia
- ▶ Ulcerative colitis

For further information on medical marijuana, you can refer to Michael Backes' *Cannabis Pharmacy: The Practical Guide to Medical Marijuana*, Jack Herer's *The Emperor Wears No Clothes: Hemp and the Marijuana Conspiracy*, or Christian Rätsch's *Marijuana Medicine: A World Tour of the Healing and Visionary Powers of Cannabis*.

A comprehensive list of 23 additional texts and scientific studies on cannabis and its medical benefits can be found at Avicanna's website: http://avicanna.com/background-information.

For an all-encompassing view of cannabis and its future, look into Steve DeAngelo's *The Cannabis Manifesto: A New Paradigm for Wellness*.

Intake Methods

Before ending this introductory chapter, let's look into intake methods, as these can influence the type of product you might wish to sell.

A very large percentage of people believe that smoking is the only way to consume marijuana. A smaller percentage have also heard about edibles and vaping. However, the number of delivery methods in existence today is much higher and so are the number of business opportunities. Check out some of the most popular intake methods in Figure 1–10 on page 24.

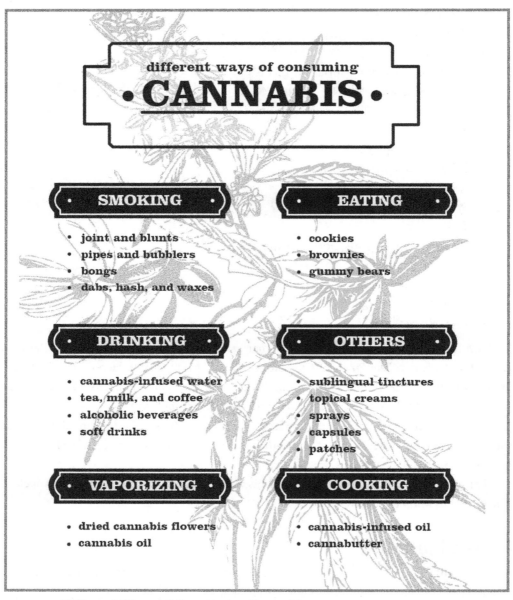

FIGURE 1–10: **Different Ways of Consuming Cannabis**
Source: Image by Agustina Yofre. Find it at http://cargocollective.com/agustinayofre.

"The fact that cannabis is usually used as a whole plant is a problem. Cannabis has close to 500 chemical constituents that interact with each other, creating an entourage effect," Yale University's Dr. Pearlson says.

"If you go to a pharmacy and buy a Tylenol, that's just one thing: acetaminophen. Whereas if you are taking cannabis as a medicine, you are taking in a whole bunch of cannabinoids, terpenoids, etc. that are very different from strain to strain," he says. So cannabis entrepreneurs have two further potential business arenas as a result: one from isolating specific compounds from the cannabis plant and the other from breeding new strains with particular chemical profiles.

Taking advantage of the fact that medical research of cannabis is easier in Canada, Avicanna has been working on developing transdermal patches, capsules, sublingual sprays, topical creams, and other delivery mechanisms based on their understanding of how cannabinoids work. "So, comprehending the benefits of cannabis and cannabinoids is the first step. The second one is understanding the most efficient delivery of those cannabinoids for different indications," CEO Aras Azadian explains, pointing out that inhalation isn't always the best method. For instance, by smoking cannabis, you don't get the topical benefits of cannabinoids, those good for your skin, which you would get by applying creams and other topical solutions.

The Rise of a New Paradigm

The traditional perception of cannabis is generally associated with flower products—or dried buds—but that's changing rapidly with the rise of new types of products.

"While flower sales still dominate with over 50 percent of the market, the growth rate of the flower category is much slower than other segments, like concentrates, pre-rolls, and vapor pens, which are showing well over 100 percent growth year over year," Leafly co-founder and Headset co-founder and CEO Cy Scott says. To illustrate the popularity of each delivery method, check out some recent information that Headset, Scott's data and analytics firm, shared in Figure 1–11 on page 26.

Figure 1–12 on page 27 shows a graph for the state of Washington alone, where Headset has more extensive data.

Finally, Table 1–3 on page 27 shows the results of a survey that online cannabis education platform Green Flower Media conducted among its most loyal subscribers—no matter where they live, showing which delivery methods people use (they could pick more than one):

"Most of the entrepreneurs are assuming flower-based products are the entry point into the market," Eric Layland, founder and principal of cannabis marketing and branding firm Canna Ventures, explains. But this approach is pretty simplistic. "In general, smoking is on the decline in the U.S. [Thus, you should] look at alternative delivery systems to smoking/dabbing. Regular consumers and new users need products that allow them to experience cannabis in a manner that they are comfortable [with]."

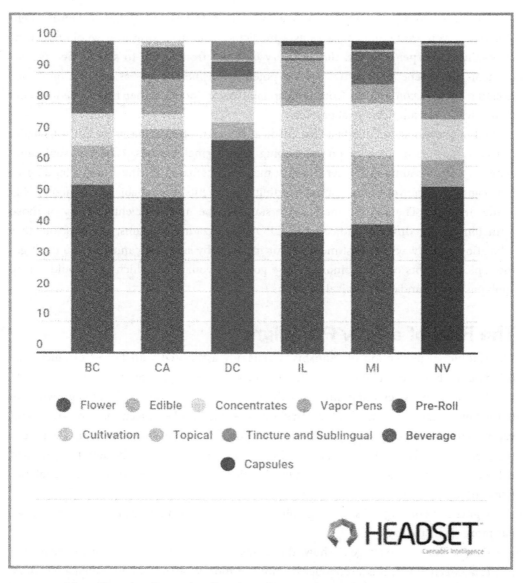

FIGURE 1–11: **Most Popular Cannabis Product Categories in Several U.S. and Canadian Jurisdictions**

Source: Headset. 2017. www.benzinga.com/news/17/09/10108982/millennials-are-smoking-less-weed-but-still-consuming-marijuana-the-rise-of-cann

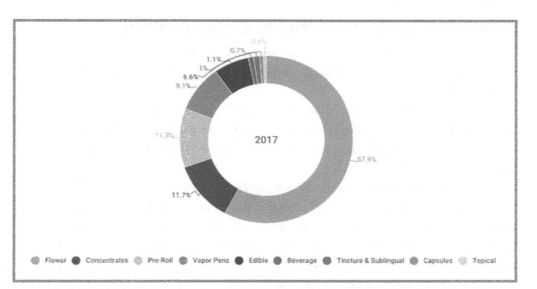

FIGURE 1–12: **Most Popular Cannabis Product Categories in Washington State**
Source: Headset. "On the Come Up: Concentrates Category Shows Consistent Growth." Find it at
http://headset.io/blog/on-the-come-up-concentrates-category-shows-consistent-growth.

Intake Method	Percentage of Respondents Using It	Number of Respondents
Pipe	53 percent	402
Joint	46 percent	352
Edible	45 percent	346
Vape Pen	36 percent	276
Portable Vaporizer	32 percent	243
Bong	28 percent	214
Tincture	24 percent	181
Topicals/Salves	22 percent	170
Dab Concentrates	17 percent	128
Desktop Vaporizer	16 percent	122

TABLE 1–3: **Green Flower Media Users General Data**
Source: Green Flower Media. 2017.

Intake Methods and Market Opportunities

Right now, the route to market for most cannabis and cannabis-derived products is through licensed marijuana retailers, although some low-dosage CBD products can be sold at regular retail stores.

However, "the future for cannabinoids is not going to be in cannabis-specific channels. It's going to be over the counter, behind the counter, pharmaceutical products, recreational products . . . They are all going to be sold in their specific places," Avicanna's Azadian predicts.

So different delivery mechanisms will be available at different retail outlets. Smokable cannabis products will likely still be sold at marijuana retailers, cannabis-based pharmaceuticals might end up being sold solely at pharmacies, and so on. This dynamic is creating (and will continue to create) different retail opportunities.

> **tip**
>
> To better understand the different forms in which a patient can consume cannabis, consider reading Ed Rosenthal's *Beyond Buds: Marijuana Extracts— Hash, Vaping, Dabbing, Edibles & Medicines.*

Another way to look at this is from a demographics standpoint. "So take the example of Whoopi & Maya's brand," Max Simon, founder and CEO of Green Flower Media, points out. "Their products are 100 percent geared toward women and predominantly women who are dealing with menstrual or pain issues. These are good products, but they are not unique in the sense that there are similar products out there. But they have managed to customize their delivery methods for this particular demographic."

Another Option: Industrial Hemp

Beyond medical and recreational marijuana, the cannabis industry also encompasses the cultivation, processing, and trade of industrial hemp, which many argue could end up having a larger economic impact than its psychoactive cousin, weed. So far, 34 states in the U.S. have hemp laws in place, allowing the production and/or research of cannabis sativa L. that contains very low levels of THC—typically below 0.3 percent.

While we could discuss the properties and potential of hemp for pages, let's keep this overview as brief as possible in order to move on to the main topic at hand: starting a cannabis business.

To make a long story short, industrial hemp, a nonpsychoactive member of the cannabis family, as its THC levels are almost negligible, can be used to make plastics, oils, fuels, fabrics, paper, and CBD-rich products, among many other things. In addition, hemp has enormous nutritional value, and its cultivation and later processing are believed to result in a carbon-negative activity. This means that, while the plant itself pulls carbon from the air, hemp products that are later discarded will biodegrade, returning carbon to the soil and replacing an element that is often drained by cultivation cycles.

For more information on industrial hemp, check out:

▶ Hasse, Javier. "Why Hemp Could Be the Future of Plastics." Benzinga (May 5, 2017). www.benzinga.com/markets/emerging-markets/17/05/9405826/why-hemp-could-be-the-future-of-plastics.

▶ Hasse, Javier. "Why Industrial Hemp Could Prove a Larger Economic Driver than Marijuana." *High Times* (September 11, 2017). https://hightimes.com/business/why-industrial-hemp-could-prove-a-larger-economic-driver-than-marijuana/.

▶ "Hemp 101: The Ecology of Hemp." Recreator (April 20, 2017). https://recreator.org/blogs/hemp-101/hemp-101-the-ecology-of-hemp.

▶ Martino, Joe. "Hemp vs Cotton: The Ultimate Showdown." Collective Evolution (July 17, 2013). www.collective-evolution.com/2013/07/17/hemp-vs-cotton-the-ultimate-showdown.

▶ O'Connell, Kit. "How Hemp Can Heal Our Soil & Why It Matters to Consumers." Ministry of Hemp (April 27, 2017). https://ministryofhemp.com/blog/hemp-soil-remediation.

In this chapter, we've looked into the main topics related to cannabis and the industry around it. You now know about its market potential, about the increasing social acceptance of marijuana, about how legislation has not caught up to this change in public opinion and perception, and about how that may affect your business.

In addition, we've gone over the main compounds present in cannabis and their diverse effects on and medical benefits for the body; the different intake methods and how each one has its own particular traits; the current legal landscape and the states where you could start a cannabis business; and even industrial hemp (briefly).

So now that you've completed our crash course in Cannabis 101, it's time to get down to business. Next up: the first major questions you should ask yourself before jumping into the marijuana industry.

The First Major Decisions

N ow that you have familiarized yourself with the basics of the cannabis plant, its history, its legal issues, and the industry around it, it's time to jump into the first major decisions you'll need to tackle as a cannabis entrepreneur.

The questions in this chapter will not only allow you to figure out if you can and should participate in the cannabis industry, but it will shape your business going forward. Answering these queries will be essential to creating your business plan and financial model, to determining your capital needs, and to applying for a license if one were needed. So take a seat, ask yourself these questions, and think about them—hard. The answers you end up with should be unequivocal and unambiguous. Are you ready?

Is This Business the Right One for You?

Support for cannabis legalization in the U.S stands at a record high. In April 2016, CBS News released a poll showing that 61 percent of Americans believe marijuana should be legal. This number rose to 64 percent by October 2017, according to a Gallup survey.

Per Gallup's conclusion, these figures demonstrate that, as the positive results of legalization become more evident in multiple states, public perception of marijuana is shifting, and the stigma around weed is being steadily overcome—largely driven by the medical marijuana movement. The only real stigma that remains today is related to cannabis' illegality, rather than to public perception, BDS Analytics' Tom Adams contends.

"Regulations around cannabis are changing rapidly around the world, along with social acceptance," says Derek Riedle, founder and CEO of the cannabis and lifestyle media company Civilized. "Think about this in the fullness of time: in a few years, opposition to cannabis will become marginalized as cannabis becomes more mainstream and people continue to realize that it is not the 'boogie man' that we have been told it is for generations."

Having said that, Viridian Capital Advisors' Scott Greiper warns that a percentage of the U.S. population still frowns on marijuana. There are legal implications as well: anyone who wants to get involved in this industry has to take on the reputational and legal risk(s) because even though numerous states have legalized it, cannabis is still a Schedule I, federally illegal drug under the Controlled Substances Act.

A Unique Business Model

On top of the risk of federal prosecution, IRS targeting, and asset seizure, cannabis entrepreneurs have to cope with the hazards of conducting a business that deals mostly in cash, since a majority of traditional financial institutions—banks, credit card issuers, and payment transaction companies—won't provide services to the industry. In addition, there are often risks surrounding transactions conducted with proceeds from what may still be considered an illegal enterprise in some areas, specifically for those who don't grow or distribute the plant. That's why security services like the ones provided by IPG become so essential.

Canna Advisors' Tyler Stratford adds that this is an industry for people with thick skin. "You need to withstand and fight against adversity in this space and be willing to help change the course forward," he says. "Be ready to be an industry operator and advocate."

No matter how progressive our society has become, we are still not completely familiar with cannabis; we are not used to having it around like we are with alcohol. So anybody who opens one of the first operations in any given jurisdiction has to be an advocate.

As an entrepreneur, you will have to "be able to explain why this is not something to be feared. Cannabis has actually been a part of our culture for thousands of years; only for a short period of time was it put into prohibition," Canna Advisors co-founder Diane Czarkowski supplements. "If you can't talk about this with people, I don't see how you are going to be successful, as you are going to keep perpetuating the same belief system."

So prepare to challenge the stigma, educate, advocate, and fight both for people's right to use cannabis and your right to run a cannabis business. The road will run uphill.

The Only Constant Is Change

Yet another question anyone evaluating an incursion into the cannabis industry needs to ponder is: are you comfortable with uncertainty and frequent change?

If not, then this nascent industry is not for you. "None of this has ever been done before," Czarkowski asserts. "Sometimes change happens so frequently that you don't have time to implement the last change before you have to make a change again."

Of course, there is one chance you will have to take as an entrepreneur starting a business in any industry: are you ready to put all your faith in your problem-solving abilities, risking your financial safety in the pursuit of a larger reward?

"You need to be able to get to the edge of the cliff and decide that you are going to jump. Since you don't always know where the landing spot is, your challenge is to build a hang glider and eventually turn that hang glider into a plane and, ultimately, a jet," Civilized's Riedle concludes.

Are You Welcome?

Another thing to consider is: are you even allowed to participate in the cannabis industry? And if so, how?

As you already know, regulations vary from one jurisdiction to another, but a lot of them will only allow people with no criminal records to partake in the industry—or touch the plant—while others will only allow state residents to start plant-touching businesses. Some add even more prerequisites: the most common are being up to date on your taxes and

▶ Moving to the Front of the Line Is No Longer a Crime

On the opposite end of the spectrum are jurisdictions like Oakland, California, which is seeking to make up for some of the harm that the war on drugs caused by giving people with marijuana-related criminal charges priority in the licensing process.

"This type of policy reflects one of the best, formidable human virtues: forgiveness, absolution," former Mexican President Vicente Fox Quesada says. "When it's correctly exercised, forgiveness can really amend our social fabric, taking away business from the hands of criminals and putting it in the hands of a community of entrepreneurs and businesspeople who will do a really good job at managing it and generating societal and economic benefits as it does.

"I see people criminalized, marginalized, suffering violence on the back of cannabis' illegality. But these people were not born criminals; the system has turned them into criminals by not providing them with access to higher education and a well-paid, decent job," he adds. "If we presented the right opportunities for these people, legal opportunities, opportunities to have a respectable life, we would be able to turn them into an asset for the economy and the country as a whole. And what better way to rescue people who suffered due to the war on drugs than by including them in the emerging legal cannabis sector, offering them decent, well-remunerated jobs?"

not having any DUIs. Find out what your state and municipal requirements are, and make certain you meet them before taking any other steps. However, if you fulfill the conditions listed above, you'll probably be fine to apply for a license.

To Touch or Not to Touch?

If, after considering all the factors above, you've decided you want to (and can) move forward with a cannabis business, the next big decision is picking a side, so to speak: do you want to touch the plant?

One would assume that businesses touching the plant bring higher risk and, thus, higher rewards. However, this is not always the case.

Risk is naturally higher when a business cultivates, sells, or even handles marijuana—and so are the complexity and rigidity of the regulations that apply to it. However, returns are not always directly proportionate to this risk. In fact, many plant-touching subsectors of the industry, like wholesale cultivation and edibles manufacturing, face problems like shrinking margins, increasing competition, and difficulty in scaling up.

Growing such businesses usually requires a lot of capital, real estate investments, new employees, and time.

That said, entrepreneurs need to remember that there is no cannabis industry without cannabis production. It is also vital to realize that plant-touching businesses are not limited to cultivation and retail—you will find a long list of business ideas later in this chapter.

No matter what type of business you choose, efficiency is key. If you can come up with a way to help make the cannabis industry more automated and more efficient, you've got yourself a business, Tyler Stratford says. "It's really about making everything more efficient, about how little you can touch the plant, and how few times can you have someone touch and move the product," he adds.

Still, you might continue to wonder about the incentives for going with a plant-touching business. Well, whiskey might help you decide.

In other words, we haven't seen the Jim Beams, Jack Daniels, and Johnny Walkers of the cannabis industry emerge yet. You could fill one of those spots—be the first to create a legacy product or brand. "Whether they are medical or recreational, there are very few brands that cross state lines nowadays. So there's a real opportunity to create a great national, and even international, brand," Stratford says.

"The biggest incentive is that, really, you can control your own destiny in a lot of ways. You are not relying or depending on the industry's growth, like being an ancillary company; you are not relying on any of the market demand outside of what you create for your own business," he adds. "On the operations side, touching the plant might be the shortest way to making money and not remaining in debt over a long time."

On the other hand, businesses that do not touch the plant often offer reduced risk and the potential for higher rewards. Think about scaling up a software company or advisory firm: it is often easier to grow and get into multiple states with these sorts of companies than it is to increase the size of a grow operation or retail location. Once the product or service is created and polished, your main job will be to grow your client base and distribution capabilities.

While the path for a business that will not touch the plant might seem easier at first, starting such a business often requires a certain level of technical and/or technological knowledge and a relatively large amount of seed capital. But this doesn't mean that nonexpert entrepreneurs should shy away from this sector, as there are plenty of nontechnical opportunities in consumption devices, physical security, marketing, public relations, event planning, media, etc. (Be patient; we're almost to the list of business ideas!) However, to whet your appetite, here's an infographic (Figure 2–1 on page 36) that illustrates how legalization can give birth to unexpected ancillary businesses.

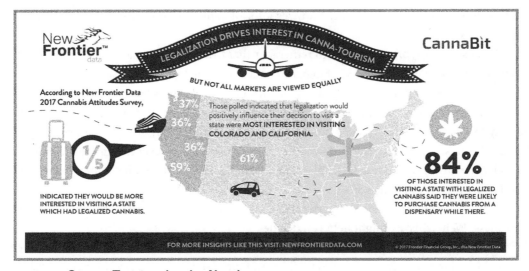

FIGURE 2–1: **Canna-Tourism by the Numbers**
Source: New Frontier Data.

Actually, if you're looking to start a business in a more mature market, meaning in a state that did not legalize cannabis very recently, the ancillary side of the industry might provide more opportunities. "All you have to figure out is what problems exist," Diane Czarkowski notes. "On the other hand, in a brand-new market, direct operators are the first to open [a business], and then it takes a little while until there is really a demand for some of those ancillary businesses, with the exception being those you'd really need at the very beginning to help the businesses run, like a security firm, record keeping, or even delivery services for moving product from one place to another."

And now the table you've been waiting for: Table 2–1 on page 37 shows a long list of possible cannabis businesses for you to consider.

> **tip** ⓘ
>
> Whether you choose to get up close with the plant or serve another sector of the cannabis market, it is essential to remember that **cannabis businesses are all about compliance.** In other words, you can't hope to succeed unless you know the rules that govern both the touch and no-touch parts of the industry.

In an industry where breakeven arrives relatively quickly, it's not making money that's the most difficult part of the job—although it's becoming harder every day. Rather, it's getting the permits to start your business and keep it operational. You will read about these aspects of a cannabis business in detail in Chapters 5 through 8.

Grow weed	Grow hemp
Sell marijuana to medical and/or recreational users	Sell paraphernalia (pipes, bongs, rolling papers, etc.)
Provide physical security	Publish a cannabis-related magazine
Start a cannabis-related website	Blow glass bongs
Make pipes or rolling papers	Cook cannabis edibles
Start a cannabis-infused foods company	Offer cannabis chef services
Organize cannabis-friendly events	Make vaporizers
Operate a cannabis-friendly hotel, hostel, or bed and breakfast (often called a bud and breakfast)	Organize dispensary and grow-operation tours—think of a classic wine tasting tour and substitute with pot
Import, manufacture, and/or sell growing equipment—lights, timers, irrigation systems, etc.	Provide specialized professional services like accounting, legal advisory, consulting, etc.
Sell a specific soil mix for cannabis cultivators	Produce organic fertilizers to help grow cannabis
Manufacture oil extraction machines	Trim cannabis flowers
Manufacture hemp consumer goods using hemp-based fabrics, plastics, etc.	Offer logistics and transportation services to wholesalers
Sell special rubber gloves for trimmers	Offer retail cannabis delivery services
Clean or wash cannabis flowers	Produce and sell seeds or plant clones
Make eco-friendly or resource-optimizing pots	Manufacture hydroponics or aeroponics systems
Produce cannabis-focused podcasts or video content	Make marijuana concentrates like hash or dabs
Offer public relations, advertising, marketing, and/or SEO services for cannabis businesses	Run cannabis-friendly activity centers offering different classes—like yoga, painting, meditation, singing, sculpting, etc.
Make and sell cannabis flower bouquets	Design cannabis-related spaces
Design packaging	Produce cannabis-specific packaging
Build greenhouses or indoor cultivation facilities	Take pictures and/or record cannabis events
Specialize in the design and/or programming of cannabis-related websites	Help with recruiting and staffing for cannabis businesses
Manufacture odorless weed containers	Offer licensed caregiver services

TABLE 2–1: **Cannabis Business Options**
Source: Green Flower Media. 2017.

Picking a Subsector

There are many subsectors in the marijuana industry. A clear categorization is the one used by Viridian Capital Advisors, which suggests dividing the space into 12 segments:

1. Agricultural technology
2. Biotechnology and pharmaceuticals
3. Consulting services
4. Consumption devices
5. Cultivation and retail
6. Hemp
7. Infused products and extracts
8. Investments and M&A
9. Miscellaneous ancillary products and services
10. Physical security
11. Real estate
12. Software and media

Some of these sectors require a lot of technical or technological knowledge and plenty of capital. For a budding entrepreneur like you, it's probably wise to focus on the most accessible ones: consulting services, cultivation, retail, hemp, infused products, extracts, physical security, and other ancillary products and services.

However, this is an industry with open doors, receptive to anyone with good intentions and a heart in the right place. Every time he talks in public, Andrew Pitsicalis, CEO and president of Purple Haze Properties, a celebrity licensing company that represents Digital Underground, Jane's Addiction, and many other artists, shares a story.

He contends that the so-called "green rush" is for everyone—not just Ivy League graduates. "You might not have the route that some groups and big-money people have, but everyone can find a niche—something that works for them," he says, arguing that people can do a lot of things around cannabis, from making edibles or growing actual flower to packaging, public relations, graphic design, marketing, and ancillary products like rolling papers.

"Cannabis users are not just going to smoke cannabis; they are going to enjoy everything around the lifestyle of that," Pitsicalis adds, bringing up his cannabis lifestyle radio, Purple Haze Radio, which officially launched in 2018 and seeks to embrace everyone in the cannabis culture and be a positive influence on this collective.

Similarly, Mehka King, director of the documentary *The Color Green: Cash, Color and Cannabis* and host of the CashColorCannabis podcast, tries to not always talk about weed on his shows. "I try to introduce entertainment, politics, and pop culture into the conversation about the cannabis sector," he says. "So you can see it's a very wide conversation that cannabis creates; it's not as narrow as people believe."

You will very likely hear a lot of "experts" say that the days when anyone could start a cannabis business are over and that the industry now wants professional entrepreneurs with proven track records migrating from other industries. But this is certainly not the case. A creative idea, a willingness to work hard, and a good team will take you very far in this flourishing field. And down community lane, never underestimate the importance of networking. As Lori Glauser, co-founder and COO at EVIO Labs, a publicly traded cannabis analytical testing and advisory services firm operating multiple labs, puts it: "There is no shortage of cannabis business conferences, networking events, and even job fairs that people can attend to learn about the industry and see the opportunities that are available. There is a huge range of companies that touch the space—not just growers and retailers, but specialty insurance, security, software, packaging and supplies, HR and payroll services, and more."

"Just like any other industry, the cannabis industry offers an enormous range of different opportunities for people to play in—from customer service jobs all the way up to concierge services and event companies. So what I'd recommend they do is find the place where they already have existing skills, an existing background, existing experience," Green Flower Media founder and CEO Max Simon concurs. "People get excited about growing or making products. But I would say it's best to stay away from these areas if they don't have any experience in this field."

In addition, make sure you are developing a special product. "Bad quality will not fly in this industry," he concludes. And cultivate a strong, reliable supply chain. This is crucial to maintaining consistent quality and preventing other people from knocking off your products.

On a final note, John Sidline, principal at public relations firm The Cannabis Story Lab, reminds us not to forget about the diversity of the cannabis user base. Don't just think about the stereotypical "stoner" when you are coming up with a product. "Remember the 80-year-old Parkinson's patient who is trying to get control of his tremors," he says, "or the soccer mom who doesn't like to have a cocktail at the end of the day but wouldn't mind to have a little bit of a buzz or something like that . . ."

If you're looking to start a business in spaces like software, agricultural technology, media, or real estate, check out some of the numerous incubators, business accelerators, and mentorship programs, like CanopyBoulder, Gateway Incubator, or Greenhouse Ventures, which have been created to guide you in this very complex endeavor and help you raise capital beyond your friends and family circles. While these programs might demand equity participation in the businesses they back and mentor, they can also help reduce consulting and advisory expenses enormously.

Realistic Possibilities

Two things are key in determining which subsector (and ultimately, which specific line of business) is the right one for you: your skill set and the competitive landscape.

Your Skills

On the aptitude side, the main questions you should ask yourself are:

- ▶ What do I know, and what don't I know? What am I good at?
- ▶ What do I have experience in? How can I apply my talents to this industry?
- ▶ What do people close to me know? Would they be willing to be a part of my team? What are they good at?

Advisors across the board often urge people to avoid changing jobs. Change your industry instead by figuring out how to make your background useful in a new field. The cannabis industry provides the perfect opportunity to do just that since it's a relatively new and emerging sector. Think about what skills you already have from your experience in other businesses that might apply in a lateral move to being a cannabis entrepreneur.

Your Competition

On the competitive landscape side, you'll need to do extensive market research to find out which subsegments are saturated in your state and which ones still have space for new businesses. Take into account that there are still a lot of unmet needs in the industry, especially when it comes to companies servicing exclusively cannabis businesses.

Take the example of Wurk: it does regular old payroll management. However, its system has been created especially for the cannabis industry. Other similar companies include:

- ▶ Baker Technologies (www.trybaker.com): customer engagement
- ▶ CanPay (www.canpaydebit.com): debit payments processing
- ▶ Green Flower Media (www.learngreenflower.com): online education
- ▶ Headset (http://headset.io): retailer-direct data
- ▶ *High Times* (https://hightimes.com), Leafly (www.leafly.com), and Herb (https://herb.co): media

▶ IPG (www.ironprotectiongroupsecurity.com): physical security
▶ Salar Media Group (www.salarmediagroup.com) and Proven Media (https://provenmediaservices.com): public relations

All these businesses do things that other, much larger companies have been doing for decades; what differentiates the firms above and drives their success is their focus on the cannabis industry.

"With good connections and a little bit of foresight of the needs this industry will create as it expands, you can create something with great potential," CannaAdvisors' Tyler Stratford says.

Location

Location is central to figuring out your market selection equation. You can either pick a location first and then determine which business is most likely to succeed there or think of a business and then find the right location for it. Do not forget, though, that many states only allow residents to start plant-touching businesses, so be sure to find out whether your state has an open or closed market.

"A cannabis business has two specific types of markets: an open market like you see in Colorado or Oregon and a closed market like you see in Florida or New York," says Kyle Speidell, co-founder and CEO of The Green Solution, a cannabis company with more than a dozen retail locations in Colorado.

An open market allows for anyone who fulfills the legal requirements to start a cannabis business to start one, no matter what state he or she was born or resides in. Conversely, a closed market only allows its own residents to start cannabis businesses. You would need to domicile there and spend a few years actually living in that state and paying taxes before you could start a business in the cannabis space. So market location analysis up front is key when determining your initial strategy.

"Everyone believes that by just getting into cannabis you will become rich, and that is far from the truth; your profitability will be determined right from the start with your market analysis," Speidell explains. "If you are in an open market, your brand will matter significantly more than a closed market, and if you do not have the strong background knowledge on how to build a brand, you will not appeal to customers that have a plethora of choices. If you are in a closed market, you will have more opportunity to succeed, even when you make mistakes, but you should use that time wisely to build something others cannot easily catch up to because your brand will matter as the market moves to an open model." Figure 2–2 on page 42 illustrates how location can determine your possibilities by showing how cannabis-friendly tourism companies are more likely to succeed in certain states or cities.

FIGURE 2-2: **Canna-Tourism Destinations**
Source: New Frontier Data.

Location can also determine which kind of business you can start in another way. "If you are, let's say, in rural Iowa, and not in an urban area like New York City, the possibility of getting involved in the cannabis industry through the production of hemp might be much easier," Electrum Partners' Leslie Bocskor adds.

A rural location like this would also be great for people seeking to make a business out of servicing hemp cultivators. If you don't want to grow hemp, you could provide farmers with the right kinds of nutrients for hemp cultivation, build greenhouses, supply lighting for indoor grows, offer clean energy options, or process the raw material to make plastics, paper, or oils. Again, the options are ample.

Take into account the existing infrastructure as well. To better illustrate this point, respected cannabis activist and successful entrepreneur Steve DeAngelo holds up his company as an example. Harborside was the first cannabis company to start growing weed in Monterey County, California. He primarily chose this location for the pre-existing infrastructure: there were unused greenhouses that could be purchased and refurbished for a reasonable price, a large unemployed workforce with experience growing and cutting flowers, and a climate that was ideal for cultivating marijuana.

"I know, from my position in Harborside, that about 80 to 90 percent of the current supply going into the legal, medical cannabis market in California is produced indoors under high-intensity lamps. And there are two issues with that mode of production,"

DeAngelo explains. "The first one is that it consumes vast amounts of energy and has a horrible carbon footprint. . . . The second problem is that growing cannabis indoors, as opposed to growing it in a greenhouse facility, is extremely expensive."

So by finding the right location in terms of climate, infrastructure, and workforce, Harborside was able to start producing cannabis that was the same or better quality as other producers for at least half the cost.

On the other hand, if you're seeking to start a cannabis business in an urban area, you'll probably be more inclined to create a lifestyle-oriented company: maybe a smokers' lounge or dispensary or a firm that makes products for cannabis users, such as bongs or pipes.

Conduct Initial Market Research

Lastly, you'll need to go back to the market research stage to determine what your target customer base or audience will look like. "Even people in the business believe that cannabis consumers stand in a straight line, but they don't," documentary filmmaker and podcaster Mehka King says.

Understanding the diversity in the market is particularly important when you are thinking of ways to reach your consumers and searching for creative and fun ways to engage them (we'll look further into this in Chapter 8, Getting the Word Out). For now, ask yourself questions like:

▶ Will you make products for men, women, or everyone?

▶ Will your client base have a Millennial skew, or will it be tilted toward baby boomers?

▶ Are you aiming at recreational users, medical patients, or both?

▶ Is your ideal customer a blue-collar worker or a white-collar worker?

▶ Does your typical customer own a car? Is he a drinker? Does he use Facebook, Instagram, Twitter, and Snapchat?

Use your answers to these questions to create a plan for setting your business up around your customer profile. "Any business that deals with the consumer, whether it's Procter & Gamble or the grocery store down the street, needs to have a plan to decide what products to carry [or make] and how to market them," says Consumer Research Around Cannabis vice president Jeffrey Stein. That plan includes figuring out who your target consumer base will be, what it will look like, what it will sound like, the age range, the income range, and so on. And this discovery process starts with consumer research, which will become increasingly indispensable as the cannabis industry continues to grow and competition surges. Let's take a look at some research stats about cannabis customers.

► What's the Word on Weed?

If you're still having trouble deciding on the right location for your business, the map from the people at DankGeek (shown in Figure 2–3 on page 45) might help. They used trends software that has access to geotagged Twitter data to uncover which U.S. states talk about cannabis more than alcohol. The results are based on more than one million geotagged tweets issued over a month-long period. The team looked at tweets for each state containing common cannabis terms (weed, marijuana, 420, etc.) and compared them with tweets containing common alcohol terms (beer, whiskey, wine, etc.).

The states that talked about weed the most were:

- ► California
- ► Nevada
- ► Georgia
- ► Texas
- ► Maryland

Also, in the following states, and only in these five, women discussed marijuana more than men did—while Twitter usage by gender is pretty balanced.

- ► Hawaii
- ► Arkansas
- ► Missouri
- ► West Virginia
- ► Wyoming

Research by Talking to Investors

Micah Tapman is a prolific marijuana investor and managing director at one of the top cannabis business accelerators, CanopyBoulder, which focuses on highly scalable, ancillary businesses in the cannabis industry. In his view, the best way to come up with a strong business idea is to start talking to investors.

While talking to customers can help you get a better idea of what the public wants, and talking to potential partners and team members can help you determine your actual possibilities, talking to investors will provide insight into what the people with the big money are willing to support.

► **What's the Word on Weed?,** continued

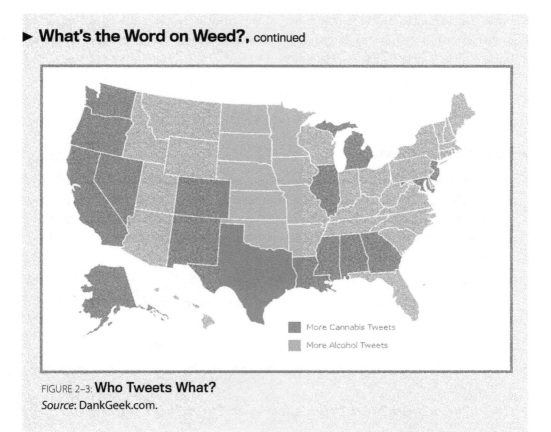

FIGURE 2–3: **Who Tweets What?**
Source: DankGeek.com.

Think of this process as writing a book. "You might do better if you start by talking to publishers before you figure out exactly what you want to write because publishers can tell you what they want to publish," Tapman suggests.

Now, translating this analogy into business lingo, imagine you reach out to 20 investors and three of them say they would love to see you work on, for example, a point-of-sales software system. Well, now you know that the odds of getting their support if you assemble a team dedicated to building that system are fairly high.

"I like to recommend you start with real conversations with investors, with building up your network, (and) with finding the people who will give you money," Tapman concludes.

Research by Working in the Trenches

One way to learn the business from the ground up is to learn on someone else's dime while collecting a paycheck. Hadley Ford is the CEO and co-founder of iAnthus

Capital Management, one of the largest investment firms in the cannabis space. Based on his experience in the industry, he proposes an alternative route to starting a marijuana business: "If you currently have a regular job outside the cannabis industry and you've had some track record of success and excellence, *the* best thing you can do to get into cannabis is to go work for a cannabis company," he says.

▶ Buyer Breakdown

Consumer Research Around Cannabis (www.consumerresearcharoundcannabis.com/) offers market insights by state and multistate data. As an example, the firm (in conjunction with Green Market Report (www.greenmarketreport.com/) shared some multistate information showing that a large percentage of the people who declared they had purchased cannabis from a legally authorized retailer:

- Have a full-time (47.1 percent) or part-time (17.1 percent) job
- Are white-collar workers (27.3 percent), business owners or managers (13.7 percent), or professionals (13.0 percent), while 10.2 percent are retired
- Are married (40.9 percent), while 34.2 percent have never been married
- Drive a Ford car (19.1 percent), Chevrolet (16.2 percent), Toyota (14.4 percent), or Honda (12.4 percent)
- Are frequent wine drinkers (23 percent) or frequent beer consumers (14 percent)
- Have a dog (60 percent) or a cat (36.7 percent)
- Have a 401(k) account (25.8 percent)
- Are white (53.8 percent), of Hispanic descent (24.8 percent), black (14.1 percent), or Asian (3.4 percent)
- Have used Facebook (81.1 percent), Instagram (52.7 percent), Pinterest (46.8 percent), Twitter (45.7 percent), or Snapchat (44.8 percent) at least once in the past month
- Subscribe to Netflix (59.2 percent), Amazon Prime (27.9 percent), or Hulu (27.4 percent)
- Visited McDonald's (43.4 percent), Taco Bell (18.3 percent), Wendy's (17.8 percent), or Burger King (17.6 percent) at least once in the past four weeks
- Drank Coca-Cola (31.2 percent), Pepsi (23.8 percent), Dr. Pepper (13 percent), Mountain Dew (12.1 percent), or Sprite (11.1 percent) at least once during the week before the poll

Source: Consumer Research Around Cannabis. 2017.

▶ Meet Jane West, Cannabis Advocate

Take all the most important things mentioned in this chapter, and you've got Jane West's story. The tale of how her brand rose to fame, of how she became one of the most prominent advocates in the cannabis industry, named "the most widely recognized female personality in cannabis" by *Inc.* magazine in 2016, is marked by the overcoming of social stigma, the embrace of the reputational and legal risk that came with getting involved in the pot space, the need to become an industry operator and advocate, the lack of seed capital, the taking advantage of a pre-existing skill set, an industry migration rather than a job change, the recognition of an unfulfilled need and the capitalization of said opportunity, and the fortune of being at the right place at the right time.

The year was 2013. Jane West, a mother of two in her 30s, lived in suburban Denver, Colorado. She had a pretty good job planning corporate events, making roughly $90,000 each year, working from home. "I loved, loved, loved this job I had held for eight years," she declares.

One night, while having dinner at a restaurant, a friend of hers (who knew she was an avid cannabis consumer) offered a marijuana-infused edible. She describes that as an amazing night, filled with laughter and joy. And so Jane's pleasant experience with weed quickly became a business idea: "Now that the recreational use of cannabis is about to become legal in Colorado, I will start hosting pot-friendly parties," she thought. "It's going to be amazing!"

A scant couple of weeks later, she decided to just go for it. "For the first time ever in my life, because both my kids had started school full time, I had free time in my hands. And, since I had been planning events for maybe 10,000 people, planning a cocktail party for 150 people at an art gallery was a fun thing to do."

And so she did. Her first cannabis event caught the attention of the food editor at *The Denver Post*, who became interested in her story, met her, attended one of her events, and decided to feature it on the first page of the newspaper's food section.

"This article was particularly huge because it ran on January 8, 2014, the weekend of legalization [in Colorado]," Jane explains. Due to this unique occurrence, every major media outlet in the U.S. had sent a reporter to Denver, so Jane decided to invite them all to one of her cannabis events. The party was a hit, Jane remembers. But when the CNBC segment on Colorado's legalization aired and heavily featured Jane, her bosses at the Washington, D.C.-based events planning firm she worked for were not at all happy. And just like that, Jane was out of a job.

▶ Meet Jane West, Cannabis Advocate, continued

"I didn't think I was going to get fired when I started this," she says. She was left with no choice but to embrace her destiny. Fortunately, demand for her services was hotter than July.

She continued on until April 2014, when the city of Denver shut down one of her events, eventually charging her with a misdemeanor. "I am now a criminal, with six criminal charges," she adds.

Legal prosecution forced Jane to transform her events into fundraisers. She was not willing to give up on her project, even if that meant making zero dollars out of it. "This new focus got us international media attention," she says.

Riding this notoriety wave, Jane and famed entrepreneur Jazmin Hupp decided to start the cannabis networking group Women Grow in August 2014, after raising $42,000 in seed capital. Soon there were chapters in nearly 50 cities nationwide, with tens of thousands of regular attendees. While the group's revenues are still catching up with its brand recognition, the venture has nonetheless proven invaluable to Jane in terms of experience and industry connections. It also helped plant the seeds of her next business venture. With Women Grow, she'd successfully helped women engage in the cannabis space as professionals. Now she saw the need to connect women consumers with cannabis.

"I was ready to do something real," she says.

From organizing so many events, Jane had noticed it was close to impossible to find bongs (a type of marijuana consumption device) that were consistent in quality and design. They were either too big, or too ugly, or too round at the bottom so they could not stand, or just too different from one another. As cannabis went mainstream and users became more sophisticated, even replacing things like wine drinking with weed consumption, there was a gap that needed filling, and Jane was determined to be the one who did that. So she reached out to Grav Labs, a company she believed was great at making cannabis-related glass products, and asked them to make a customized, Jane West-branded line of marijuana consumption devices—which now generate millions of dollars in sales a year.

Their advice and input were fundamental, Jane recognizes. So was their help in getting her product to market, and her brand name and logo really out there. Following the success of her initial product line with Grav Labs, the Jane West Collection, her team's first line of proprietary smoking accessories, has been conceived for women, and holds the potential to revolutionize the way women see cannabis.

To learn more about Jane and get more exclusive quotes from her, read the full story at http://entm.ag/26j.

"Because there is a dearth of capital and there is a dearth of good people, you can prepare a good resume and get hired in the middle management of some big operation. . . . work nine-to-five for six to 12 months, and learn the business from the inside and see what it takes to launch your own business in the space," Hadley Ford adds.

In addition to learning the nuances of your specific subsector, getting a job in an existing cannabis company can help you understand the challenges all cannabis businesses face. It can ultimately become a differentiator when raising capital for your own business because, unlike many other prospective cannabis business owners, you'll have experience in the sector.

Talking about how EVIO Labs hires, co-founder and COO Lori Glauser adds, "From entry-level couriers and cannabis samplers, analytical chemists, and biologists all the way up to senior executives with experience growing a business and running multiple labs and technical personnel . . . most of our employees came to EVIO with little or no prior cannabis testing experience since cannabis testing is a relatively new business. In fact, some have never consumed (or very rarely consume) cannabis. We don't necessarily look within the cannabis industry for our candidates as cannabis science can be learned. We bring professional scientists and customer service-oriented people from a variety of industries."

"Even if you decide to raise money from your Uncle John, by getting a job, you'll have a good answer when he asks what you know about cannabis," Ford comments.

If you already have a job in this industry, congratulations! You're way ahead of the curve! If not, and if you have the ability to move away from an existing job in another industry, make the move and get learning.

The
Initial
Planning

O nce you've conceived the basics of your business-to-be, you should move on to coming up with an appropriate, skilled team and a realistic business plan and financial model. There is a lot more than you might imagine between having an idea and actually being able to execute it.

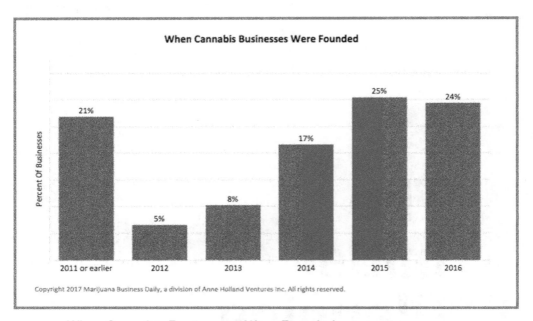

When Cannabis Businesses Were Founded

FIGURE 3–1: **When Cannabis Businesses Were Founded**
Source: Marijuana Business Daily's "Marijuana Business Factbook 2017."

"This is a very deep rabbit hole," Electrum Partners' Leslie Bocskor warns in a humorous tone. However, don't get cold feet. People have been founding cannabis businesses and running them successfully for years, as Figure 3–1 shows. It's definitely not too late to get aboard.

One recommendation that generates wide consensus among experts is the need for a lawyer and a CPA. These professionals will prove instrumental to preparing your business plan and financial model, as well as to determining your capital needs, legal obligations, and potential challenges and benefits of operating in this industry. Moreover, a CPA will not only keep your books, but also will help you make all kinds of important decisions, like if you should lease or buy equipment.

"Lawyers and CPAs are essential. This is something that I tell people interested in getting into the cannabis

tip

Before doing anything else, find a co-founder, someone who supplements your abilities and knowledge, and will support you, as almost every person interviewed for this book suggested. Take time to evaluate your potential partners and pick them wisely; make sure you have shared goals and values. Uncountable cannabis businesses have failed on the back of disagreements between partners.

industry and people migrating from the black market or what we call 'grey market,' which is an unregulated medical market. Regulations in this industry change very rapidly, and you need to keep up with them. A CPA and an attorney are your best side dogs in shepherding you through all these changes and keeping you current," says Anne Van Leynseele, a lawyer at 7 Point Law specializing in the cannabis industry, who was named as one of the Top Women Attorneys in 2017 by *Seattle Met* magazine. This is a highly regulated, complex business. Never forget this!

> **tip** ⓘ
>
> NORML offers a directory of attorneys servicing the cannabis industry at their site: http://lawyers.norml.org.

In addition, take into account that, while a business lawyer can do some of the work, a cannabis company needs an attorney or firm experienced in cannabis who will be a lot more familiar with all the risk factors involved in operating in such a multifaceted industry. So try to find lawyers who have been working in the marijuana space for a while.

"There are a lot of lawyers out there who have never done what you are asking them to do as a company," Van Leynseele says, suggesting you ask them how many cannabis clients they have worked with when picking your counsel, as they are legally obliged to answer sincerely.

Getting Started

Keeping those broad suggestions in mind, it's time to jump into the planning phase. The first thing you will want to ask yourself during the initial planning stage is **Who will run this business?**

This might seem like a ridiculous question at first, but it is not. Many entrepreneurs already have other businesses or day jobs, so they don't have much time left to run their new cannabis business. At some point, they'll be faced with the decision of quitting their day jobs or getting someone else to run their marijuana business.

If you will run the business, you're clear to move on to the next step of the initial planning. However, if you won't be in charge of everyday operations, you'll need to find someone suited for the endeavor.

It's a good idea to start with the people around you for those key positions. Find out what they are good at, and make them a part of your initial team. Remember that experience in the cannabis industry is not necessary, although it is always a plus. Depending on the size of your new business, you might consider who will take on the following roles:

▶ Someone who will deal with investors, banks, taxes, and other financial issues

- Someone who will deal with providers, vendors, and potential clients
- Someone who will hire and manage your personnel
- Someone who will take care of your initial communications
- Someone who will help you with all your business planning and general operational issues
- Someone who will handle your business' security

Returning to the issue of finding a partner, Jay Czarkowski, co-founder of Canna Advisors, explicates that "every person has [their] own strengths. So maybe if you're a good salesperson but you're not very strong on the financial side, you might want to go out and find a co-founder who's strong financially or vice versa."

Once you've identified the right people for your team, you'll need to define exactly what you want to accomplish with your business. Diane Czarkowski remarks: "You can't open a dispensary and not really have a feel for what the experience will be like. Will you be a combination of a sort of doctor's office and a high-end coffee shop? Or will you want to be a convenient, get-out-the-door-quickly dispensary? Or will you go for a value-driven experience, offering the best prices in town?" These are things you need to decide beforehand.

The third step in this early planning is to conduct a deeper analysis of the competitive landscape. In this line, employing techniques like the SWOT (strengths, weaknesses, opportunities, and threats) analysis might prove effective.

Finally, you'll have to decide if and how you will want to scale your business. What's the end game? Do you want to eventually get acquired by a larger company? Do you aspire to go public? What are your long-term goals? All these are important questions to ask yourself as you map out a mission statement and business plan.

The Mission Statement

Before going any further, you will want to clearly define your company's mission. This will help you remain focused and not get diverted by all the ideas that constantly arise during the process of building a business—especially in an industry as new and all-encompassing as cannabis. In other words, come up with a few phrases that unequivocally state what your company does and what it wants to be doing in the future. You can ask yourself questions like these to help parse out your mission. Do you want to:

- Become the king of edibles?
- Become the number-one producer of cannabis in your state?

▶ Run the leading cannabis oils company?

▶ Break ground as the first cannabis-focused human resources agency in your region?

Narrow your focus to set your mission apart and avoid the pitfall of trying to be all things to all cannabis customers. "The lack of focus in the cannabis industry is world-renowned," Cameron Forni, co-founder and president of Cura Cannabis Solutions, one of the largest marijuana companies in the U.S., points out. "It is absolutely amazing how people can want to own everything from grow operations to processing plants, to edibles manufacturing facilities, to retail stores, to limos that come and pick people up and drive them around retail stores, to advertising companies that advertise in the limos . . . In the end, people get this paralysis from all these new ventures and ideas and products and segments."

Matt Gray, founder and CEO of HERB, the most engaged cannabis community on social media, says, "People don't buy what you do; they buy *why* you do it. Doesn't matter if you are a dispensary, a producer, or a product brand. What's most important to the consumer is to know that *you* care." Of course, the way you communicate this is deeply intertwined with who your customer is. You should know who you want to make products for or offer services to by now (see more on this topic in Chapter 2).

To further illustrate his point, Gray points to HERB's mission. After seeing a friend who had gone through a traumatic experience that had him on the verge of suicide recuperate using cannabis, Gray decided to start a platform aimed at educating users on the benefits of marijuana. "From day one, our mission has been to smash the stigma around cannabis and to show people the magnificent potential of this plant," he says.

"Having my *why* clear has allowed me to build a great company, a strong community, and a magnificent team. Once people know *why* you are doing what you are doing, they will be ready to care about what you do and how you do it."

So before moving on to a more formal business plan, ask yourself why you want to get into the cannabis business—beyond just making money. What do you want to accomplish, and why?

Run the resulting statement past the people close to you and ask them if it makes sense to them, if your mission is clear enough, and if it generates any kind of emotion. If your family and friends, people who are not necessarily involved in the cannabis industry, can grasp what you want to accomplish, your team will likely be able to do so as well.

Next, we'll look into the main elements involved in coming up with a viable business plan to pitch to investors, support your operations, and even butter up regulators.

Getting to Know the Business Plan

Probably the most important element of your business' initial development is the business plan. One vital reason for creating a business plan derives from the necessity to raise capital: you need something to show potential investors, even if they are friends and family members.

"If you have family and friends who are willing to invest in you and your dream, that is very helpful, of course, but it's also a lot of responsibility. You will owe it to these people to perform well," Cannabis Culture's Jodie Emery says.

Based on the extensive experience that Electrum Partners' Leslie Bocskor has in helping people build businesses, he advises you to really focus on the due diligence and business plan parts of the startup phase. "Most businesses fail because they did not conduct the proper research before they started," he says.

"We cannot stress enough the importance of research, hard work, being good at money management, research, and more research when you are starting a business," Daniel Cheine, co-founder of the cannabis-focused social network, advertising platform, and knowledge database CannaSOS, agrees.

An ideal business plan should provide an overview of the market and include your business' vision and mission. Viridian Capital Advisors' Scott Greiper suggests a few other questions you might want to answer as you craft a plan:

- ▶ What's your go-to-market strategy? What kind of channel will you pick: direct or indirect?
- ▶ Will revenue come from one-time transactions, or will it be recurring?
- ▶ What is the level of price competition in the market, and have you factored that competition into your business model?
- ▶ Can gross/operating margins be maintained in a downward pricing environment?
- ▶ What are your ongoing capital requirements relative to your increase or decrease in burn?
- ▶ Will growth be organic or is marketing and advertising an important component of the overall growth strategy?

For investors, the viability of your business model is fundamental, Greiper, who has helped raise more than $500 million for emerging growth companies, adds. For instance, you should pay close attention to pricing pressures. Never assume the pricing for your product (whether it is a piece of software, an extraction technology, a lighting system, or even packaging) will remain static or increase over the next few years. In the current environment, you will most likely be wrong.

"This is a hypercompetitive environment right now," Greiper says. "So the metrics that you put in your business plan and financial model have to be relevant and current with the facts on the ground, [basically factoring in] a continued decline in wholesale prices and increased and better-funded competition that is coming in with better management teams."

However, a business plan is intended not only to show investors the profitability potential of your enterprise but also to show regulators how your business will benefit the community. To that end, consider the following:

▶ How many jobs will you create?
▶ Will you benefit any minorities or marginalized communities?
▶ Will your store, office, or production facility be located in an economically disadvantaged area?
▶ Will you help sick people?
▶ Will you have a positive impact on the opioids epidemic?

Once you've done some strong self-examination, you can sit down to craft a plan. A typical business plan will include the following:

▶ *Executive summary.* This is a short yet enticing summary of the business. Although it usually appears first, this section is often written last—after you have put all the other pieces of the plan in place.
▶ *Product/service description.* Here you include specifics about what you are selling, why it is a viable idea, and what goes into the production.
▶ *Industry analysis.* Remember everything we discussed in Chapters 1 and 2? Investors want to know those industry basics, too. Talk about the big picture of cannabis, and back up your statements with facts and numbers.
▶ *Competitive analysis.* Who is competing in your product/service space? This is where you lay out what you do differently and how you do it better than the other guy.
▶ *Marketing and sales.* Here you talk about your plans for getting the word out about your business. How will you promote the product? Where will you advertise? How will you sell it? Do you plan to use traditional or more conceptual types of marketing?
▶ *Management.* In this section, you tell readers who is running the show. Potential financial backers are particularly interested in this information because they want to know to whom they are entrusting their money. Include all the key people involved with day-to-day operations. If this is a solo venture, include a bio that features your applicable experience.

► *Operations.* How does that day-to-day work get done? This part of the plan details the "how" of the business. The specifics will depend on whether you are selling a product or service, operating a storefront or online store, or partnering with a related company.

► *Financials.* The goal here, with the help of your accountant, is to make realistic projections based on researching similar businesses and then specifying what you think you'll need in terms of financing. Because this section is so vital to your success, it is covered in greater detail on the next page.

► Is a Business Plan Really Necessary?

While many investors and finance experts will assure you that a business plan is absolutely essential, others, like CanopyBoulder's Micah Tapman, believe it is completely useless.

It no longer makes sense for startups to come up with an old-fashioned business plan, Tapman contends. A plan is something that family and friends usually want to see, but more sophisticated investors are increasingly looking for something else. "You know that you don't know most of the stuff that you need to know," he says. "So what you need is an outline, not a full plan."

Other things Tapman believes you need to build a business, instead of a business plan, are:

► Confidence, to be willing to start down the path to owning a business

► Humility, to recognize that your assumptions and beliefs will often be wrong

► Mental agility, to change things in your plan as you learn and evolve

Tapman says there is *one* thing you certainly won't know during the planning phase, and that is how your business will operate.

Let's say you are planning to start a logistics company, providing transportation and storage services to cannabis companies in California. Most likely, you won't know much about this business at first: you can find out how much it costs to buy a truck and lease a warehouse but not much more.

"Most investors today, I think, are happy to see a business plan in the form of a PowerPoint presentation that is 15 or 20 slides long, covering the basics of what you are trying to do, and a short spreadsheet," Tapman says. "We want to know things like if you have factored the cost of your trucks' insurance. Now things like if you are going to buy or lease trucks, I don't care at this point. The fact is you can't predict this."

For more detailed information on what to include in your business plan, check out Entrepreneur's book *Write Your Business Plan.*

The Financial Plan

Most business owners recommend you get professional help when putting a business plan together. For the financial part, seek out an accounting pro like a CPA. For the legal side of things, it's never too early to hire a lawyer. Just like monthly health insurance premiums can save you thousands of dollars when you get sick, being compliant from the start can avoid huge litigation expenses down the line.

A financial plan is fundamental to any startup. In this document, you will assess your current and future assets, liabilities, income, net worth, asset allocation, financial goals, reinvestment plans and targets, tax deductions, real estate costs, and so on. In addition, a good, strong, farsighted financial plan often includes an exit strategy, a way to sell at least part of your business once it's big enough; this might be an outright sale or an IPO at a major stock exchange, among other options.

Some of the elements you need to include in your financial plan are:

▶ Your real estate costs and whether you are better off renting or buying a property

▶ The key people running the business and how much they will make

▶ Your construction costs

▶ Your operational costs

▶ Your advisory expenses

> **tip**
>
> Make sure you have enough money in your budget for professional financial and legal advice. Prepare to spend $15,000 to $20,000 a year on your legal counsel, cannabis lawyer Anne Van Leynseele says. In addition, beware of so-called "financial advisors," as the term is meaningless— basically anyone can call him or herself that. Play it safe and hire a trained professional, like a CPA or a CFA.

According to Marijuana Business Daily's "Marijuana Business Factbook 2017," the cost of starting a cannabis business varies widely depending on the sector. So, while starting an ancillary services firm has a median cost of $15,000, opening a testing lab costs about $700,000. Dispensaries stand somewhere in the middle, with a median startup cost of $192,500.

Median operating expenses also vary considerably, ranging from $72,000 a year for ancillary services firms to $900,000 for dispensaries. Check out complete data sets in Marijuana Business Daily's report.

► What's Your Worth?

In 2017, HempStaff, a leader in legal cannabis recruiting and dispensary training, shared a data set showing average salaries for certain cannabis professionals by state:

Alaska

► Cultivation manager: $70,000 to $80,000 per year

Arizona

► Dispensary agent: $10 to $12 per hour

California

► Trimmer: $10.00 to $12.50 per hour

► Dispensary manager: $45,000 to $60,000 per year

► Extraction manager: $80,000 to $100,000 per year

► Assistant grower: $40,000 to $60,000 per year

► Master grower: $100,000 per year

Colorado

► Master extractor: $52,000 to $70,000 per year

► Master grower: $70,000 to $100,000 per year

► Office manager: $35,000 to $40,000 per year

► Dispensary agent: $10 to $13 per hour

Illinois

► Dispensary agent: $12 to $15 per hour

► Agent in charge: $15 to $20 per hour

► Master grower: $85,000 to $95,000 per year

To provide further context, the report also goes into median annual revenue and average net profit margins for these businesses. So, for instance, ancillary services firms generate about $100,000 in revenue per year and get a 31 percent margin, while dispensaries have median annual sales of $1.7 million at a 19 percent net profit margin. Take into account that these figures can vary widely from state to state, partially due to large differences between effective tax rates and labor costs. Also take into account that the people you hire will have an enormous impact on your financial plan and overall

▶ **What's Your Worth?,** continued

Maryland

- ▶ Master grower: $120,000 per year
- ▶ Dispensary agent: $12 to $14 per hour

Massachusetts

- ▶ Master grower: $120,000 per year

Ohio

- ▶ Master grower: $100,000 to $120,000 per year

Oregon

- ▶ Dispensary agent: $11 to $12 per hour
- ▶ Dispensary manager: $30,000 to $45,000 per year

Pennsylvania

- ▶ Master grower: $75,000 to $120,000 per year
- ▶ Extraction manager: $75,000 to $85,000 per year
- ▶ Compliance officer: $75,000 to $85,000 per year

Rhode Island

- ▶ Master grower: $80,000 to $100,000 per year

Washington

- ▶ Assistant grower: $25,000 to $40,000 per year

Source: HempStaff Salary Data, 2017.

profitability. The cannabis industry pays very well, and you will need to offer salaries comparable to the national average. Check out the sidebar on page 60 to get a feel for how much cannabis employees can earn.

Ultimately, being able to start a successful business boils down to knowing how and when to ask for help. If you have no idea how to raise money, get advice. If you don't know everything about the product or service you will offer, get advice. If you aren't a legal expert, get advice. Always get advice from real experts—the people who have been working in the industry for years.

Tax Code 280E

The most (or only) boring thing about cannabis, and probably about modern-day life, is paying taxes. And taxes for marijuana businesses are even more complex than they are for most companies. Consequently, most seasoned cannabis business owners will strongly advise you to hire a CPA to do your taxes and ensure your business remains compliant.

You can find a directory of CPAs servicing marijuana businesses at either of these two links:

1. www.ganjapreneur.com/marijuana-accounting-firms
2. https://industrydirectory.mjbizdaily.com/accounting

Despite getting professional help, if you will be touching the plant, you need to know about one particular regulation: § 280E, found in the U.S. tax code under Title 26, Subtitle A, Chapter 1, Subchapter B, Part IX. This regulation concerns the deductions you will be able to make and thus the effective tax rate that will apply to your business.

In most businesses, you can deduct, among other things, salaries, wages, transportation and car expenses, equipment, supplies, furniture, legal expenses, professional fees, rent, depreciation of equipment, utilities, repairs, insurance, advertising, travel costs, many types of commissions, meals, interest from business loans and mortgages, retirement plans, software, and other service subscriptions from your taxes.

However, businesses profiting from the sale of cannabis cannot. Due to marijuana's continuing federal illegality, cannabis businesses can only deduct the cost of goods sold and, in some cases, expenses derived from the provision of caregiving or medical services. This means that the effective tax rate for cannabis businesses is a lot higher than usual, sometimes reaching 45 percent. Some business owners even report they have been charged up to 70 percent of sales in taxes.

"Because of the tax code 280E, you can't make any business deductions besides cost of goods and one inventory person. So everything from rent, utilities, salaries, and advertising to paperclips, printers, and computers, you can't deduct," explains Brendan Hill, drummer for the band Blues Traveler and cannabis impresario. "So even a store like Paper & Leaf [his dispensary on Bainbridge Island, Washington], which generates $4 million or $5 million in revenue per year, can only deduct our cost of goods, which is probably a third of this number, but all the other expenses are basically taxed."

In some cases, plant-touching businesses that have losses on the books still have to pay taxes, GreenWave Advisors' Matt Karnes, a CPA, adds. Ancillary businesses, though, are treated like regular businesses and can take their deductions normally.

► Location, Location, Location

Location is one of those things you need to pay close attention to when starting a cannabis business. Where you decide to set up your business will have a huge impact on your prospects, and thus your business plan and financial model.

In order to find the place that is right for you, you will have to evaluate numerous factors, including zoning issues; proximity to schools, public parks, child-care centers, churches, libraries, rehab centers, community-service agencies, and other public spaces; water rights; energy rights; infrastructure; applicable taxes; how the licensing process works; and, of course, lease or purchase costs.

Take into account that, when renting, landlords have to explicitly agree (usually in writing) to have a cannabis business operate in their property. In addition, the real estate in question cannot have a mortgage on it.

"Upon finding out that a cannabis company is in residence, either by lease or by ownership, a mortgage provider can call the entire mortgage in 30 days," cannabis attorney Anne Van Leynseele explains.

Other fundamental things to know are your land use rights and what your water source will be as well as how much water you will be able to use and what your water runoff requirements are. These elements are critical and very often overlooked.

Go-to-Market Strategies

One of the elements you should consider during the startup phase is the go-to-market strategy, which includes things like how you will sell your product or service in an industry as localized and fragmented as the cannabis industry. Are you going to knock on the doors of thousands of dispensaries and growers? Are you going to focus only on direct sales? Ultimately, how will your product or service reach your customers?

Keep in mind that each customer segment can be most easily reached in a particular way. So before going any further, you need to know which segment each customer group comprises and figure out if you can reach them all. Here are a few strategies to consider:

- ► Direct sales
- ► Indirect sales through partners and distributors
- ► Joint ventures
- ► Online sales

"The direct sales model is often the most profitable because there is no middleman, but it is also usually the most expensive because you will have to hire a lot of salespeople to go knocking on doors and making phone calls," Viridian Capital Advisors' Scott Greiper explains. "So there should always be, in my opinion, an indirect sales strategy as well, whether that's a website that can take orders, whether that's a distribution company that will take your product and distribute it among hundreds of businesses in their network.

"You need to develop relationships with people within the industry who can represent your product," he adds. "This is the cheapest customer acquisition strategy, albeit not the most profitable."

In this line, one important thing to consider is conflict. Make sure your diverse sales channels do not overlap; this will confuse your employees and customers.

Your Legal Status

One last thing you should decide during the initial planning phase, before moving on to raising capital, getting a license, and setting up shop, is your legal status going forward. In other words, decide what kind of organization you want to set up to protect your personal assets in case something goes wrong with your business.

"How you establish the organization of your company is essential in your success down the road," Anne Van Leynseele explains. Solid foundation documents are key in this process. "Even if it's a single person, every company needs to establish either an LLC, a general liability partnership, or a corporation for personal protection."

Notice that sole proprietorships are somewhat problematic because they *do* allow creditors to claim some of your personal assets to cover company debt. "Even if you think you don't own very much, as you build your business you will start to have personal assets that would make it worthwhile for someone to reach out and grab those," Van Leynseele points out.

Another part of creating a useful, sound operational agreement is clearly outlining each partner's roles and responsibilities. It is common to see partners failing to make their initial investments or fulfill certain obligations when these are not explicit contractual requirements.

Entity formation is also key to sound tax planning, Bradley Blommer of Green Light Law Group adds. "Regulations like the IRS' 280E [tax code] are applicable to certain licensees more than others. So getting a good CPA who is an expert in the 280E is crucial for anyone starting a new cannabis business," he concludes.

▶ Meet Andy Williams, Serial Cannabis Entrepreneur

Consider the story of Andy Williams, co-star of MSNBC's *Pot Barons of Colorado* and serial cannabis entrepreneur. In just a few years, Andy and his brother Pete built a marijuana empire that includes Medicine Man Denver, one of the largest and best-ranked cannabis dispensaries in the U.S.; Medicine Man Technologies, a marijuana industry consulting services and solution management company that trades over the counter under the MDCL symbol; an intellectual property holding company; and a real estate holding company, among others.

Growing up, Andy and Pete were far from affluent. They had, nonetheless, managed to build relatively decent careers for themselves. Andy, an industrial engineer who had not been very lucky with his business ventures in the past, had made it to the management levels of the corporate world. Meanwhile, Pete had set up a custom tile company, but to make ends meet, he also worked as a caregiver, helping medical marijuana patients in Colorado.

Being in constant contact with cannabis and having a knack for inventions, Pete had come up with his own system for growing marijuana and was making pretty good money from selling pot. Nonetheless, growing weed illegally in his basement was not ideal. So Andy and Pete put a business plan together and decided to pitch it to their mom, Michelle, and her husband, Lou Zeman, even though the pair had never used cannabis before, or expressed any interest in the industry. It seems the couple liked the proposal, because they quickly agreed to put in $150,000 in seed capital.

The initial business plan the Williams brothers came up with included financial projections for three years. "They were very detailed, month-to-month forecasts for each year," Andy notes. "Our projections were based on how the market looked at the time, what we projected the market would be, how much [cannabis] we could grow, etc. . . . Five years later, my brother Pete decided to compare these projections with the actual numbers, and they were pretty damn close."

With $150,000, the siblings set out to find a physical location for their company-to-be, Medicine Man. The first big problem the Williams brothers encountered was real estate. Even though vacancy rates in Denver were pretty high at the time, nobody was willing to rent out their space to a marijuana grow operation. After an extensive search, they finally came across a 40,000-square-foot building in Montbello—an industrial area in northeast Denver—which was partly occupied by a spice company. The smell the factory emanated made the remainder of the property undesirable to almost any entrepreneur. But Medicine Man's business would be no stranger to strong odors either.

▶ **Meet Andy Williams, Serial Cannabis Entrepreneur,** continued

The remainder of this pot baron's story is pretty well known. After two very successful years in operation, Medicine Man bought the entire building, forcing the spice factory to move elsewhere.

Due to state regulations, the Williams brothers were quickly required to get into the retail side of the cannabis industry as well. This vertical integration ended up being fundamental in the construction of a brand that now enjoys not only statewide but also nationwide recognition—if not fame.

Capitalizing on that good name, Andy, Pete, and a business associate and now friend, Brett Roper, started another company in 2014: Medicine Man Technologies. As the brothers' companies continued to expand, they branched out into other endeavors: an intellectual property holding company, a real estate holding firm, a cannabis processing and research company, and even a business that invests in cannabis businesses and helps them go public on major stock exchanges. In addition, Andy and Pete are extremely committed to "the fight to protect the industry from those who want it dismantled and the fight to normalize the industry at the local, state, and federal levels." They are often a part of the cannabis-related legislative process in their home state of Colorado.

For the full story behind Andy, Pete, and Medicine Man, including exclusive quotes, visit http://entm.ag/x5j.

The time to start building your business has finally come. Before doing anything else, get a good lawyer and a good CPA, identify the key people who will be part of your team, and decide who will run your business.

Once you have these basics established, you can move on to creating a mission statement, a business plan, and a financial model. In addition, this is the time to get acquainted with all the rules and regulations that apply to the business and location you've chosen; remember that there will always be multiple levels of regulations and, on occasion, these might even conflict. So, again, you should get help from a professional in navigating these turbulent waters.

The number-one thing to keep in mind from this point forward is this: Always remain compliant with the law. The slightest error might doom your business for good.

The Financing Issue

Kevin Harrington, the original host of ABC's *Shark Tank*, is often regarded as the creator of the info-mercial. Having sold more than $5 billion worth of products over his career, he is frequently invited to talk about business and entrepreneurship.

During a conversation in September of 2017, Harrington revealed that whenever he asks the entrepreneurs in the audience at any of his events if they will need to raise capital at some point in the near future, only maybe 10 to 20 percent raise their hands.

"So the rest of you are financially independent and have all the money you are ever going to need for your business?" he challenges the attendees. Suddenly, all hands go up.

This anecdote illustrates pretty clearly a problem that is common to most entrepreneurs in any industry: the disregard for the need to raise capital. People often believe that they will be able to put only a little money into starting a business and they will not only recover it quickly but also start making a profit in no time.

However, it is more likely than not that your own money will not be enough to even start your business. So let's take a look at how to raise capital for your company-to-be.

"Just like with any other business, if you are going to be raising money, any investor will be concerned with three things: number one, how much money are you raising; number two, how will you use that money; and number three (and this is the most important), how will he or she get his or her money back," Canna Advisors' Jay Czarkowski contends. Consequently, the first thing you need to do is come up with a clear plan to pay your investors back.

Also central to this process is getting your capital needs right. What if you go out and raise $1 million, which seems like a lot, and it ends up not being enough? What if you actually need $1.5 million?

Think about the Williams brothers: they thought they'd need a lot less money than they ended up requiring. They were fortunate enough to be surrounded by people with the financial means and the willingness to support their venture and its evolving needs. But not everyone can be as lucky.

As you read in Chapter 3, getting off to a strong financial start really begins with having a good business plan to show potential investors. But financing is also about reaching out to as many people as possible. A pristine business plan and financial model are worthless if nobody gets to see them.

"We tried to get funding from venture capitalists, from the crowd, from private investors, seed investors, angel investors," CannaSOS co-founder and CEO Oleg Cheine comments. "We sent out like 20,000 emails."

The bottom line is that entrepreneurs have to be persistent. "There is nothing like persistence. Good investors will appreciate that and thank you for insisting down the road," financial marketing veteran Hugh Austin concludes.

The Banking Problem

So what about banking? Can a cannabis business head down to the local bank and set up a checking account like any other business? The answer, it turns out, is complicated. Leaving more complex services like investment banking aside, commercial banks offer two basic products: credit and everyday banking, which includes checking accounts.

Due to the federal illegality of marijuana, almost no banks in the U.S. offer credit to the industry. In fact, access to capital is mostly limited to so-called "private mortgages" or private investors—think venture capital funds or family offices.

On the other hand, there are regular old banking services. Again, some of them, like issuing or processing credit card payments, are not available to most cannabis businesses— regardless of whether they are in contact with the plant. However, some other services, like ownership and use of a bank account, are accessible; in fact, many businesses and investors in the industry say they would never transact with a company with no bank account. Check out Figure 4–1 to see just how difficult it is for a cannabis business to access traditional banking avenues.

Access to bank accounts is clearly becoming more widespread, as you can see below. Still, it's harder to get a bank account for a cannabis business than for any other legal business out there—and the difficulty increases for plant-touching companies. Notably, this limited access is not because financial institutions are not allowed to service the pot industry but because many of them are unwilling to face the risk or additional regulatory burden of doing so.

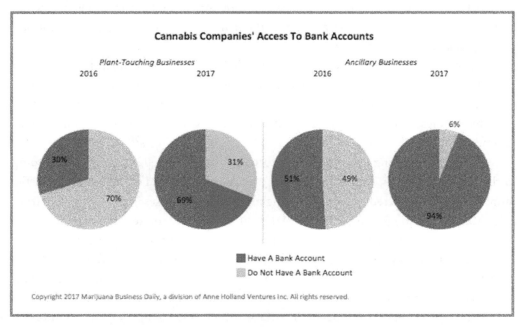

FIGURE 4–1: **Cannabis Companies' Access to Bank Accounts**
Source: Marijuana Business Daily's "Marijuana Business Factbook 2017."

"All banking and financial services legitimately participating in the cannabis industry must be able to prove to state and federal regulators that their cannabis clients comply with the law," says Dustin Eide, CEO of CanPay, the first debit payment network built specifically for compliant cannabis dispensaries. "It's a high bar, and most institutions and services do not want to go through the extra work and expense required to be in compliance."

"The due diligence, reporting, and oversight associated with providing banking services to cannabis businesses is costly; banks do not have the appetite to become investigative entities, which leads to the current catch-22 situation," Giadha Aguirre de Carcer, founder and CEO of New Frontier Data, explains. "The cannabis industry is currently primarily cash based, leading to significant lack of transactional transparency, leading to banks fearing money-laundering risk, leading to banks not wanting to provide services, leading to the industry remaining cash-based—a true conundrum and one likely to only go away if the industry becomes federally legal or if state-based compliance and reporting standards improve significantly."

So what does this mean for you? What should a cannabis entrepreneur do to find capital? For the time being, several alternatives to traditional banks (like credit unions and specialized firms providing banking services) have emerged to service the industry. As of early 2017, 13 percent of ancillary businesses and 34 percent of plant-touching businesses in the industry received services from a credit union instead of a traditional bank, according to Marijuana Business Daily's Factbook.

"The community banks and credit unions see banking in the cannabis industry as a community safety issue, first and foremost. They should receive all due credit for building programs that are intended to make their communities safer by eliminating the need for cannabis businesses to transact in cash and carry that cash around in their communities," Eide adds.

Luckily, the banking situation seems to be getting a lot better. Actually, according to the Associated Press, data from the U.S. Department of the Treasury shows that the number of banks and credit unions servicing marijuana businesses in the U.S. spiked from 51 in March 2014 to more than 300 by March 2016. However, more often than not, these institutions charge cannabis businesses higher-than-usual fees for their services.

Check out a listing of financial institutions that service the cannabis industry at https://industrydirectory.mjbizdaily.com/banking-point-of-sale and at www.ganjapreneur.com/cannabis-banking-payment-processing.

Despite the increasing number of financial institutions servicing the cannabis industry, credit is still very rarely available for marijuana businesses.

► Debt vs. Equity

Before moving on, here is some cautionary advice: be careful how you fund your company.

"Back in 2014, most companies were raising debt. No matter what kind of debt, the fact of the matter is that, for an emerging growth company without a lot of existing revenues, cash flow, or big backlog of forward revenues, you may be in a position where you can't either service the debt and keep it current, or pay off the debt when it comes due," Viridian Capital Advisors' Scott Greiper explains. "And this is a real problem because then someone else will own your company."

Note that the data in Table 4–1 below represents the capital raised by global cannabis-related companies captured by Viridian Capital Advisors' Cannabis Deal Tracker market intelligence initiative and may not be entirely comprehensive.

In USD Millions	Total	Equity	Debt
2014	$148.2	$129.7	$18.6
2015	$905.3	$839.8	$65.4
2016	$1,292.6	$1,049.4	$243.2
2017	$3,498.4	$2,853.7	$644.7

TABLE 4–1: **Cannabis Capital**
Source: Data shared exclusively by Viridian Capital Advisors.

This said, funding a company with equity is not easy, but you should at least try to do so.

"Getting funding for a cannabis business presents very unique challenges because you can't just get an SBA or small business loan, and banks are not going to lend money to you either," Super Bowl champion turned cannabis entrepreneur and investor Marvin Washington explains. "Unless you are migrating, leaving your career at Wall Street or Silicon Valley—which a lot of people have done—and have a nest egg, you will have to go through nontraditional routes to get your financing."

So where exactly does an entrepreneur turn for funding? Let's explore some important topics related to getting your cannabis cash in place.

Seed Capital and Series "A" Raises

Your first (or seed) capital round will, more likely than not, be completed with money from family and friends or personal savings prior to your market debut. Although this limits your options, this is the reality of the industry nowadays since traditional funding for cannabis startups can be hard to come by.

The second (or Series A) round, which takes place sometime after your launch, may attract professional, third-party investors, after you have managed to accumulate a few pilot or regular customers.

"A seed round is aimed at building a product, service, or technology and getting some early traction, typically in the form of beta or pilot customers," Viridian Capital Advisors' Scott Greiper says. "This will help you establish some reference cases. Investors will want references from clients in the future.

"A Series A round is for moving into normal operations and your initial scale-up: hiring more people, broadening your product line, ramping up sales and marketing efforts, coming up with more distribution agreements, maybe even some initial PR, so you can get some articles, press releases, and visibility," he says.

One final note: while family and friends will take common stock in your company in exchange for their hard-earned money, professional investors will most often look for some kind of additional benefit.

"Early-stage investors investing in startup companies typically invest in preferred stock. It's not common stock, which gets to sit with every common shareholder; they have certain special rights like a dividend payment, interest payment . . ." Greiper adds. "So the early-stage entrepreneur should be raising his or her first tranches of capital in the form of equity and is likely to see preferred equity as the first type of professional money that is being offered."

Valuation

The other big concept an entrepreneur needs to understand before going out to raise capital is how valuation works.

Simply put, your company's valuation is equal to its net worth or what a sensible buyer would be willing to pay for it. You may not know this, but in the early days, your company's valuation is often determined by how much equity you need to give out in exchange for the money you get, rather than by an actual calculation of its potential value. At first, there aren't many other simple ways to value your company.

So imagine you go and raise $50,000 and give your investor 5 percent of your company in exchange for it. There, you just got a $1 million valuation. If instead you manage to raise $200,000 from your friends and family and end up distributing 10 percent of your company among them, you just went to market at a $2 million valuation.

Calculating the real value of your company is difficult, and it often means having to set your ego aside. However, take into account that, if someone is offering $50,000 for 5 percent of your company, which you haven't even started yet, they are basically implying that your idea is at least a million-dollar idea. So whether or not you ultimately agree with the terms of the investment, take that valuation as a compliment.

Another important thing to remember is to never base your valuation solely on those of your competitors. Nothing ensures that 1) their business model is actually similar to yours, even if it seems that way, and 2) they were valued correctly.

"You can't grow a business with valuation," Scott Greiper comments. "You grow a business with capital.

"And underneath that is even a more significant point. Getting a seed round done at the right valuation is not only important to bring in the right investors and try to minimize dilution but also to show future investors how you manage, invest, and capitalize on the money people give you—how you use it to grow your business."

Some investors suggest there is even merit and strategic thinking behind taking a lower valuation than you would like for your seed or Series A rounds. "If you price your first rounds right and generate strong returns for your investors, your chances of getting a higher valuation, more capital, and better investors in your later rounds get significantly enhanced," Greiper concludes.

Think of it as hiring a stockbroker. If he gets your first trade right, you are more likely to stick with him, even if he misses the target in your second or third trade, because he managed to make you money fast.

Small-business loans are not available for cannabis businesses. So where will you get the money you need to start a business?

Before we look at the diverse funding alternatives available, you should remember to be careful with the way in which you choose to finance your company, to get comfortable with the fact that its valuation will be determined by others, and to reconcile with the idea of going to your friends and family for the first round of capital.

Now it's time to look at the different people and firms investing in the cannabis industry. In the following chapter, we'll take a look at the main steps you should take to approach the investors pouring money into cannabis businesses. From family offices to venture capitalists, there are things all investors value and others that are very specific to each type.

In general, investors like to see:

▶ More than one founder
▶ A strong management team
▶ A scalable business idea
▶ People committed to the cannabis industry and movement

So, without further ado, let's dig into funding alternatives.

Funding Alternatives

Since banks and traditional financial institutions do not generally offer loans to cannabis businesses, many cannabis entrepreneurs fall back on family members and friends for seed capital—and this is probably the best choice. Nonetheless, not everyone is surrounded by affluent people willing to make risky investments. And, even among those who are, many would rather not mix their personal and professional lives.

Below you'll find some other common funding alternatives for the cannabis industry, which might come in handy when raising seed capital or when looking for additional funds for your business after a friends and family round. Not every one of them will be right for your business, though. The type of business you are trying to finance and the way you do it are intrinsically intertwined.

Hadley Ford of iAnthus Capital Management proposes an analogy. Imagine you want to get into the alcohol business: "You can open a bar, you can become a vintner, you can launch a new vodka brand. . . . It's the same thing in cannabis."

Regardless of the business you want to start, there are a few things that are common to every financing process. The first one, always, is having or opening a bank account of your own.

After that, consider turning to family members and friends for your initial capital. "Even though you may not want to go to a family member, the fact is that the biggest issue anyone writing checks ever has is trust: the question of whether you are going to be good at what you say you are good at—of whether you'll be able to execute," Ford says.

> **tip**
>
> Make sure that every investment you get is compliant with state and federal securities laws and find out about the limitations for out-of-state investors.

"The people in your own circle, in your own community, have a better appreciation of these issues. So that is the first circle of money, as it were."

"Also keep in mind that you can offer some of your initial employees equity in your company as part of their pay, saving cash at first. This is what we did with our company," Oleg Cheine and Daniel Cheine, co-founders of CannaSOS, add—although many other experts strongly advise you avoid giving equity to your employees for very diverse reasons, from avoiding dilution to fully retaining your ability to decide if and when to sell your business.

Many cannabis entrepreneurs and investors recommend you raise capital from the very beginning. However, others have argued that developing your company before getting investors in can help you go to market with a better valuation and avoid having third parties involved in the development of your brand. "A lot of investors ask for too much equity in your company in relation to the money they offer," recognized cannabis journalist Debra Borchardt says, based on her years of covering the industry's financing processes.

Think hard about how you want the investor/entrepreneur relationship to shake out in the long run before deciding on what funding source is best for you. Let's explore some more of those possible sources next.

Family Offices

Outside family members and friends, another recurring source of capital for cannabis businesses is family offices. A family office is a private wealth management firm, similar to a hedge fund, but serving just one or a few very wealthy families and high-net-worth individuals. However, getting their attention is not easy; everyone wants their hard-earned money, but few are considered worthy of it.

If you decide to go this way, try to attend family office-focused events; while most of these are invite-only, a little googling can lead you to some events open to the public. An intermediary firm with connections in the family offices space will facilitate introductions, help you with pitches, and get you invites to the right events. However, these firms tend to avoid brokering deals. A few such firms are:

▶ SCN Corporate Connect (www.smallcapnation.com)
▶ Family Office Networks (https://familyofficenetworks.com)
▶ Cavendish Global (http://cavendishglobal.com)
▶ Family Office Club (http://familyoffices.com)

"What we do is prepare the company and its CEO to get a very focused, nonpromotional message across to family offices," Hugh Austin, CEO and founder of SCN Corporate Connect, explains. "The deal we have with family offices is that we will minimize the amount of time they have to spend learning the basics about a potential investment. So instead of sending them document after document, we send a five- or six-minute video and, maybe, a short deck highlighting the company's revenues, if its management team is special, whatever sets it apart."

This does not mean that any company paying these firms' fees will get an automatic introduction to these sophisticated investors. It's important to maintain a good relationship with family offices and retain their trust, SCN Corporate Connect's managing director Bryan Crane adds. "We don't take just any deal to them. These unique sources of capital want to see high-quality deals and often shy away from friends and family rounds. So we try to take them Series A and Series B rounds," he notes.

In addition, family offices are inclined to invest in businesses with clean balance sheets and no toxic financing, which are either "cash flowing or on an obvious path to be cash flowing," Crane says.

Having said this, a new business can also explore this route. "A lot of family offices are not crazy about public companies. In fact, we've noticed that private cannabis companies have higher odds of picking a family office's interest," Austin says. "Now, these guys know they have earned their stripes, so they rarely do seed rounds—unless they offer tremendous upside.

"So if I had a cannabis company of my own, what I would do is get involved with any angel investing group that has relationships with family offices because family offices often hobble around them to see which companies make it through their filters. This is a great way to get family offices interested in a seed round," he continues. "Other great options are accelerators, incubators, and universities in general."

As responses from family offices come in, firms like SCN Corporate Connect will evaluate the level of interest and either set up a luncheon with several family offices and the company raising money or organize one-on-one interviews with a few families, coaching the raising entity's management team through the process.

Alternatively, some family offices and high-net-worth individuals pour their money into impact (or socially responsible) investments; this means that they seek business opportunities that can not only generate strong capital returns but that can also have a positive impact on society as a whole—or at least in the community in which they will operate. So if your company will benefit the environment, help marginalized communities, provide medicinal cannabis to war veterans suffering from PTSD, employ a large number of Hispanics and black people, etc., you might be able to appeal to these types of investors.

Funds, Angel Investors, and Individuals

Beyond family members, friends, and single- or multi-family offices, you might find support in some of the entities and people listed below, who have been or will be investing in the cannabis industry. There are quite a few specialized investment groups that work with cannabis startups. Though this is by no means an exhaustive list, it will get you started on your road to funding research. First you can look into specialized venture capital funds, angel investing organizations, and private equity firms like:

- ► Ackrell Capital: www.ackrell.com
- ► Angel investors from Angel.co's directory: https://angel.co
- ► The Arcview Group: https://arcviewgroup.com
- ► Benchmark Capital: www.benchmark.com
- ► Canna Angels: https://cannaangelsllc.com
- ► Casa Verde Capital: www.casaverdecapital.com

- ▶ Floris Funds: http://florisfunds.com
- ▶ Founders Fund: http://foundersfund.com
- ▶ Green Growth Investments: www.greengrowthinvestments.com
- ▶ Ground Zero Ventures: http://groundzeroventures.com
- ▶ Halley Venture Partners: https://www.halleyvp.com
- ▶ Hamilton Investment Partners: http://hamiltoninvestment.com
- ▶ Liquid 2 Ventures: http://liquid2.vc
- ▶ Mazakali: http://mazakali.com
- ▶ MedMen: https://medmen.com
- ▶ Merida Capital Partners: www.meridacap.com
- ▶ Navy Capital: www.navycapital.com
- ▶ Phyto Partners: www.phytopartners.com
- ▶ Poseidon Asset Management: https://poseidonassetmanagement.com
- ▶ Privateer Holdings: www.privateerholdings.com
- ▶ Salveo Capital: www.salveocapital.com
- ▶ Tress Capital: www.tresscapital.com
- ▶ Tuatara Capital: www.tuataracapital.com
- ▶ Viridian Capital Advisors: www.viridianca.com

You can also check out industry-specific holding companies like:

- ▶ AmeriCann (OTC:ACAN): http://americann.co
- ▶ The Cronos Group (CVE:MJN) (NASDAQ:CRONPRMCF) (FRA:7CI): http://thecronosgroup.com
- ▶ Diego Pellicer Worldwide (OTC:DPWW): www.diego-pellicer.com
- ▶ Doyen Elements: www.doyenelementsus.com
- ▶ General Cannabis (OTC:CANN): www.generalcann.com
- ▶ Golden Leaf Holdings (CSE:GLH) (OTC:GLDFF): http://goldenleafholdings.com
- ▶ iAnthus Capital Holdings (CNSX:IAN) (OTC:ITHUF) (FRA:2IA): www.ianthus-capital.com
- ▶ Innovative Industrial Properties (NYSE:IIPR): www.innovativeindustrialproper-ties.com
- ▶ MassRoots (OTC:MSRT): www.massroots.com/investors
- ▶ MJIC Inc.: www.mjic.com

Just as family offices do, the funds, organizations, and firms mentioned above also have a set of criteria that businesses need to fulfill to even get their attention. So let's look at what these investors want to see in a company when considering an investment.

► Welcome to Hollyweed

Cannabis investment goes well beyond traditional funding sources. The rich and famous are getting into the game and making serious inroads into cannabis companies in which they believe. Take a look at some of the best-known celebrities who have put their money behind the industry.

Musicians

- ► Rapper B-Real
- ► Singer/songwriter Melissa Etheridge
- ► Rapper The Game
- ► Rapper Ghostface Killah
- ► Rapper Gail Gotti
- ► Rock drummer Brendan Hill
- ► Rapper Kurupt
- ► Reggae musicians Damian, Julian, and Stephen Marley
- ► Rapper Method Man
- ► Country music icon Willie Nelson
- ► Rapper Redman
- ► Rapper Snoop Dogg
- ► R&B artist The Weeknd
- ► Rapper Wiz Khalifa

Athletes

- ► Former NFL offensive lineman Eben Britton
- ► Former NCAA running back Treyous Jarrells
- ► Tour de France cyclist Floyd Landis
- ► Former NFL defensive lineman Leonard Marshall
- ► Former NFL wide receiver Grant Mattos
- ► Former NFL offensive tackle Eugene Monroe
- ► Former NFL quarterback Joe Montana
- ► Former NFL quarterback Rodney Peete

▶ **Welcome to Hollyweed,** continued

  ▶ Former NBA player Oscar Robertson

  ▶ Former NBA player Cliff Robinson

  ▶ NFL defensive end Frostee Rucker

  ▶ Former NFL defensive end Shaun Smith

  ▶ Former NFL defensive end Marvin Washington

  ▶ Former NFL running back Ricky Williams

Other Celebrities

  ▶ Actress Roseanne Barr

  ▶ Former chairman of the Seminole Tribe of Florida and alligator wrestler Jim Billie

  ▶ Virgin Group founder Sir Richard Branson

  ▶ Comedian Margaret Cho

  ▶ Comedian Tommy Chong

  ▶ Reality TV star Bethenny Frankel

  ▶ Award-winning actress Whoopi Goldberg

  ▶ Award-winning actor Woody Harrelson

  ▶ Actress and singer Holly Robinson Peete

  ▶ Actor/director Kevin Smith, aka Silent Bob

  ▶ SuicideGirls co-founder Missy Suicide

  ▶ Beauty queen and reality TV star Jessica VerSteeg

  ▶ TV actor and talk show host Montel Williams

  ▶ *Law & Order* franchise creator Dick Wolf

Before you go knocking on doors in the Hollywood Hills to ask for money (which you shouldn't do, actually), do your research. You never know—some of these celebs or their companies may still be looking to invest in emerging cannabis businesses.

What Investors Want to See

Marvin Washington, a former NFL player turned prominent cannabis investor with stakes in six different companies, gets corporate decks all the time. The first thing he looks for in a company when considering an investment is a good business structure.

"I also like to see a solid team, formed by people who have already had success in the corporate world," he says.

However, what's most important to Washington is that the business helps people even if it doesn't make a lot of money at first.

Pointing to his investments and involvement in Isodiol and Montel Williams' Lenitiv Labs as examples, he comments: "It's fundamental to put patients first, to make sure that whatever you are selling meets the standard. Cannabis is medicine, so you should always put patients and people over profit, and make sure you are doing everything the right way and not taking any shortcuts, because there isn't much room for error in this emerging space and industry. If something goes wrong, it will taint the whole industry."

Washington's attention is on the long-term potential of a business. "At the beginning, a lot of people throw around profit projections that do not make sense," he says. "For me, however, this is a long play."

On a similar note, NFL superstar Joe Montana's motivation to invest in cannabis companies is all about educating the public on the medicinal benefits of cannabis. "Through Liquid 2 Ventures, I have invested in cannabis companies such as HERB, a cannabis technology platform, so consumers have a place to find credible information," he says.

"Being able to properly communicate your vision for the company pushes investors into your company," CannaSOS's Daniel Cheine advises.

"As industries mature, you find that the small and medium businesses become incubation labs for the acquisition targets that grow the larger businesses," Sturges Karban, CEO of MJIC, one of the largest vertically integrated operational companies in the industry, argues.

Other investors, like Phyto Partners, take a more traditional approach to investing, picking companies that are easily scalable and provide what they call "business-to-business critical solutions." Taking into account the capital needed to scale a plant-touching company, and the scrutiny these businesses are under, the firm tends to avoid plant-touching businesses.

Phyto's founder and managing partner Larry Schnurmacher says: "I don't want to grow or sell marijuana. I want to invest in the companies that are the technology infrastructure and backbone of the industry. I see companies that help licensed operators comply with the laws, provide quality and safety testing, produce excellent product at lower costs, manage human resources, retain and communicate with their customers, streamline inventory and distribution, grow technology as the best positioned to succeed in an ever-changing and fast-growing industry."

In addition, "licensed growers and dispensaries are challenged by intense competition, supply demand and pricing issues, unfair tax treatment, high costs to comply with state and federal laws, and the risk, albeit minor, of the DEA closing their business if they make a misstep," Schnurmacher continues. "The licensed growers and retailers cannot operate without the support of the companies we invest in."

CanopyBoulder's Micah Tapman adds, "Generally speaking, investors don't want to risk their money if the idea is not big enough—scalable enough. I think this is the number-one reason for a good business to fail to attract financing; the team can be good, the business can be solid, you can have a clear path to making money, everything can be A-OK, but investors still won't see this as a big win."

Let's say you are writing a book. Will you write something aimed solely at 23-year-olds in Iowa who have a college degree in Old English? Who would publish such a book? Even if it's great, the audience consists of at most 100 people.

There is one caveat to this scenario, though, Tapman adds. "Some businesses are cash-flow positive, meaning they are just going to start making money from day one. That is a little bit of an exception to the rule: they don't have to be all that big if they are going to make money, which is unusual because most businesses take a long time to start making money. But you can find *some* investors willing to put money into cash-flowing operations."

The main things investors want to see in a business when considering an investment are:

▶ A good business structure and realistic financial plan
▶ A solid team, especially on the management level
▶ A strong commitment to legal compliance
▶ Allegiance to the cannabis movement
▶ A scalable business idea with potential to become a multimillion-dollar company
▶ A founder with a good vision

One final thing investors like Tapman like to see is some kind of competitive advantage. "After finding the right idea, you need to come up with a little bit of a competitive advantage. It doesn't need to be huge; there are plenty of businesses that have a slight competitive advantage that end up doing really well," he says.

In the end, it all boils down to having confidence that your business will succeed. "Building a business is very much about belief and faith in your ability (and your team's ability) to execute and to be successful," Tapman voices.

"Once you have a vision and a strong belief in it, it's much easier to inspire people and motivate people and have them join you in the quest for that vision no matter your level of education or previous business experience," Cura Cannabis Solutions' co-founder and president Cameron Forni concurs. "If you know where you are strong, you can make sure to focus on this and then bring in the right team members to supplement any of your weaknesses."

Follow the Leaders

Douglas A.P. Hamilton is the co-founder and managing partner at Hamilton Investment Partners, a firm that has put millions of dollars into a few vertically integrated cannabis companies—including a multimillion-dollar stake in a market-leading cannabis tech firm with branded products. After explaining that he is not attracted to cannabis as an asset class but rather to the fantastic characteristics of the industry and opportunity, he emphasizes the importance of an experienced and proven management team. "There are lots of smart people whose prior experience is in staff or consulting roles, but there is no substitute for having run something in the past," he says. If you don't have experience running a business, we suggest you try to find a partner who does. This will considerably increase your odds of attracting outside investors.

Interestingly, Hamilton brings up an issue that one would expect to encounter more often: having skin in the game.

"I really want to see a financial investment (as much as can be scraped together) from senior management," he says. "If this is really a great opportunity, management should be willing to put their own money behind it."

One unique approach is that of iAnthus Capital Holdings, a firm that trades (or, in other words, raises money) in Canadian stock exchanges, where investors are more inclined to buy into cannabis companies, and then invests in U.S. marijuana companies through a U.S.-based subsidiary, iAnthus Capital Management. Also unlike most of its large investment peers, iAnthus tends to invest in businesses that touch the plant, like cultivators or retailers.

"We are an operator and look to either acquire or partner with people who have licenses. That's our bar: you have to have a license," Hadley Ford explains. iAnthus finds additional value in companies that have also proved to be "great operators or have a track record of excellence. Since finding people who have been running legal cannabis businesses for a while is rare, we often have to look at other factors of success."

For instance, one of the companies that piqued iAnthus' interest is run by a man who migrated from the pharmaceutical industry, having founded a company and grown it to a business with $50 million in sales—mostly from compounded drugs. "That sounds a lot like running a medical marijuana dispensary, where you have to determine what type of medicine is going to be best used for the affliction that your patient has—very much like a compounding pharmacist," Ford notes.

Similarly, Hamilton tends to look for a couple of years of operating results. "While startups present the greatest upside in future success, I am happy to forgo that in exchange for demonstrated success in launching the business," he explains. "While generating a profit can be a challenge in the startup phase, I need to see profitable operations going forward." This means that, while some investors will be willing to invest in your startup, assuming a higher risk in exchange for a higher potential reward, others will only give you money once you've shown you're capable of doing a good, consistent job at running your company.

Finally, Hamilton mentions the balance sheet. A positive net worth is a desirable attribute. You don't need a large net worth to catch his eye, but including contingent liabilities, a company's net worth should be positive.

So you could say it's pretty common for many of the investment firms mentioned above to invest in businesses that are already operational, rather than to go for businesses in a pre-revenue phase.

However, for some of the entrepreneurs interviewed for this book, it's best to start with your own money and some credit card debt and then go through all the stages of raising capital: family and friends, angel investors, and then funds.

"Immediately trying to get to high-net-worth individuals or funds is very, very difficult. A step-by-step progression where you find a co-founder, get a proof of concept, and make it something real (either get a product out or at least show a license) is the way to go," an experienced executive who preferred to go unnamed said.

Having said all this, note that some entities like Floris Funds *will* fund early stage businesses. "Based on our investment criteria, we are somewhat agnostic on the entity stage. That said, early stage and existing operations seem to lead the pack, likely as a result of the lack of licensing associated with seed stage opportunities," president Skip Motsenbocker declares.

So what exactly are Floris' investment criteria?

"We research opportunities using three key criteria," Motsenbocker explains. First, the Floris team investigates whether the owner or operator is trustworthy and honest. "While this may seem like a given, considering the history of the industry, it's the most important question.

"Second, we will only invest in entities that are legal and regulated both at a state and local municipal level. Lastly, we will consider the operating metrics of the business in determining the investment opportunity and acquisition valuation. These metrics are scored against our internal process to determine which businesses have the greatest likelihood for superior long-term performance," he concludes.

So when preparing your pitch to potential investors, be sure to hit these notes:

- Trustworthiness
- Honesty in business dealings
- Full, across-the-board legal and tax compliance
- State and municipality permits
- Key operational metrics in place, such as top-line revenue, operating performance relative to the expenses, and bottom line/EBIT
- Accounting practices that properly reflect the IRS' 280E guidelines

Have these pieces of the financing puzzle in place, and you have a better than decent shot at making your case for funding.

Accelerators as Unique Financers

The prescriptions above apply to getting money from friends, family, venture capital funds, private investment firms, high-net-worth individuals, family offices, and holding companies. But there are some other alternatives left. Among the remaining options are mentorship-driven programs, also called business accelerators or incubators.

Some of the top cannabis business accelerators and incubators are:

- CanopyBoulder: www.canopyboulder.com/home
- Canopy San Diego: http://canopysd.com
- Freedom Leaf: www.freedomleaf.com
- Gateway Incubator: www.gtwy.co

In addition to these specialized incubators, you might want to consider traditional accelerators like:

- 500 Startups: https://500.co
- The Launch Incubator: www.launchincubator.co
- Y Combinator: www.ycombinator.com

All three of these accelerators have admitted cannabis businesses before and might be willing to do so again as the marijuana industry continues to move toward the mainstream.

As you might imagine, each program has different requirements and offers very diverse forms of support. Nonetheless, accelerators and incubators often accept and fund ventures that are not as mature as one would expect; the idea behind many of these programs is to find good entrepreneurs and help them form and execute on their vision.

The cannabis space is great for the incubator and accelerator model, Gateway's co-founder and managing partner Ben Larson argues. "There are a lot of unsophisticated founders and a lot of venture capital looking to come in and capitalize on the space," he says. "But there is a massive gap in between the sophistication of the founders and the expectations of the venture capitalists."

One thing that both Larson and CanopyBoulder's Micah Tapman agree on is the fact that there is still a lot of opportunity left for innovation in the marijuana industry. Beyond that, their views differ substantially. In the next couple of sections, we'll take a closer look at these two very different models so you can get a better feel for what going down the accelerator route might look like.

The Canopy Model

CanopyBoulder, arguably the best-known accelerator in the cannabis industry, does not ask candidates for a business plan. All the team will solicit is a short pitch, a sort of deck or business outline showing the essential points of your business idea, your founding team, and your vision for the future of your company. What they want to see, basically, is that you have an idea that can grow into a multimillion-dollar business and that you have some sense of how you plan to make this happen.

There are a few minor caveats, though. For starters, CanopyBoulder invests only in ancillary products and services, meaning it never admits businesses growing, processing, testing, selling, or touching the marijuana plant or its derivatives in any way.

The incubator provides the businesses selected in each cohort seed funding of $30,000 to $80,000, a 16-week accelerator program, and mentor-driven training. In exchange, they ask for a 6 percent to 9.5 percent equity stake. This means that any company admitted into the program automatically gets a valuation of at least half a million dollars.

If you think you meet CanopyBoulder's criteria and are interested in its program, here are some tips to help your application succeed—straight from Tapman's mouth:

- ▶ Find a co-founder to complement your weaknesses.
- ▶ Have conversations with potential customers before applying to get an idea of the demand your product or service could generate.
- ▶ Have a clear idea of who your competitors will be and how you will differentiate from them—even if it's a small difference.
- ▶ Find the ideal geographical spot for your company to succeed.
- ▶ Try and find some kind of technological advantage, something that is a little bit different, a little bit interesting.

▶ Assemble an exceptional team that is likely to drive the success of your company. This is by far the most important element in a CanopyBoulder applicant.

"As I've mentioned before, we want to make sure that you are confident but humble, that you have done some research, and that you are tackling an idea that is big enough for us to be interested," Tapman adds. "If your business is, at maximum, going to be a $5 million per year business, it could potentially sell for $10 million or $15 million. That is probably not a big enough idea for us as investors even if it is a great idea. As investors, we will want a business that sells for $50 million, or $100 million, or $1 billion somewhere down the road."

Again, a good team is the top priority for CanopyBoulder. "We can work with a good team with a bad idea because I feel like we can discuss and fix this idea—make it better while maintaining its essence," Tapman says.

Dozens of companies have already gone through CanopyBoulder's incubator. Here are a few notable graduates:

▶ Cannabis business intelligence and market research firm BDS Analytics: www.bdsanalytics.com
▶ Agricultural technology company Front Range Biosciences: www.frontrangebio.com
▶ Automatic growing systems manufacturer Leaf: www.getleaf.co
▶ Cannabis jobs platform Paragon: www.joinparagon.us
▶ Dispensary directory PotGuide: https://potguide.com
▶ Cannabis storage and transportation systems manufacturer Stashlogix: www.stashlogix.com
▶ Cannabis workforce management platform Wurk: www.enjoywurk.com

As you can see, these businesses represent a wide variety of cannabis-related goods and services—proving that there is no one perfect road map to reach your entrepreneurial destination. An accelerator saw enough potential in all these concepts to make an investment. Who's to say your idea can't work, too?

The Gateway Model

Unlike CanopyBoulder, Gateway supports all types of cannabis businesses, whether they are touching the plant or not. However, the differences do not end here. Businesses accepted into Gateway's program get an upfront investment of $50,000 in exchange for a 5 percent equity stake in the company—implying a valuation of $1 million.

Some of the companies Gateway has mentored include:

▶ Adventure pipes maker Arc: https://arcpipes.com

▶ Trimmers-finding app Field: https://fieldapp.co

▶ Cannabis-infused brownies maker Good Co-Op: https://www.good-coop.com

▶ Artificial intelligence powered aeroponics systems manufacturer GrowX: www.f6s.com/growx

▶ Cannabis edibles maker Kamala: www.hellokamala.com

▶ Digital money platform Metal: www.metalpay.com

▶ Nutraceuticals creator Mighty Foods: www.mightyfoods.co

▶ Wellness consulting and e-commerce platform Octavia Wellness: www.octaviawellness.com

▶ Ready-to-drink cannabis-infused coffee maker Somatik: www.somatik.us

▶ Seed-to-sale management software provider Trellis: www.trellisgrows.com

▶ Vaporizers maker Uptoke: https://uptoke.net

To be considered for the program, you must submit an application explaining why you chose to do whatever it is you plan to do and what you'll be building.

"But what we really want to see is people connect with the product," Larson says. So in addition to the basic signup form, Gateway requests a three-minute pitch video that shows you're emotionally invested in your product.

"Passion is important for what the job founders are doing. But the real reason for us to look for founders who are emotionally tied to their products is because running a company is *really* hard," Larson adds. "It doesn't matter if you are the best entrepreneur in the world, if you have the best idea in the world, and all those planets are aligned: you are going to go through dark days. And the only way you are going to stick with it and continue to forge ahead and build a great company is if you are tied to solving the problem; not to building the idea that is in your head, but to solving the problems you encounter."

After that, assuming you are selected, you'll go through a phone interview where the Gateway team will evaluate if you, personally, are a good fit for their program. If that goes well, the penultimate step is the face-to-face interview. Prepare to be poked and put on your heels: The team will be evaluating how you react to criticism, advice, and the prospect of changing your original business idea.

Lastly, you'll undergo a formal evaluation, a personality and knowledge test somewhere between a Graduate Management Admission Test (GMAT) and a Myers-Briggs Type Indicator questionnaire. Beyond detecting any potential problems in each entrepreneur's personality, this examination is designed to evaluate how the co-founders (if there is more than one founder, which, by the way, Gateway almost always prefers) balance and complement each other.

If you make it past the interview process, Gateway's program is also a bit different from CanopyBoulder's in that it lasts six months and is individually tailored for each company.

"We have worked away from the classroom setting. We bring companies on as we find them and see fit [instead of by cohorts] and then create a custom program around them with the mentors and advisors that are going to really help take the business to the next level," Larson says. "We found that the classroom setting was not ideal for the entrepreneur's time. It might be great for marketing, it might be efficient for the general partners as far as the time goes, but it is really not what the companies need."

During the mentorship period, Gateway focuses on getting the companies well-structured and on setting strong foundations underneath them, Larson says. Once that period is over, the accelerator's venture capital arm, if you will, evaluates how the companies are doing and decides if they need further coaching or if they will invest some more money and help them conduct a raise among outside investors.

Each accelerator has its own unique way of helping businesses reach their full potential. If you conclude that accelerators are a good fit for your business, you should ask yourself which one is best for your particular idea. Don't be afraid to ask questions. Mentors like humble yet confident entrepreneurs.

Picking Mentors' Minds

The Gateway team believes that the largest opportunity in the marijuana industry nowadays does not stem from unmet needs but from strong founders. "Fortunately, as the stigma drops, as we do a better job of demystifying the plant, we have more successful people coming into the industry, and they are going to start doing quite well," Larson comments.

The other big thing Gateway looks for in a company, after the founders' emotional connection to their product, is scalability, even beyond the cannabis industry—both in terms of possibilities and of the founders' willingness to scale. "It's not that we think that scalable companies are the only good companies to build," Larson says. "It's just that this is what we are good at, and this is what venture capital is built around."

Here are some additional answers to our questions Larson provided that might help you fully understand Gateway's investment criteria and accordingly shape a business idea to use when you are pitching to an accelerator:

Q: Imagine you get a founder who knows how to blow glass and wants to start a glass bongs company. Would you accept him or her into your accelerator?

A: Probably not. Unless they have the concept of "blowing glass creates X product, which is better than any other product out there because it solves a problem for the consumer better than anything else." I think that is the critical question that any accelerator should ask; I think that is what makes an idea scalable. If the company actually solves a problem and the entrepreneur understands who the customer is and what he is looking for, then we would consider an investment.

Q: *What other elements would help you decide in favor of a certain company?*

A: The best and main question is: why are you doing this? In other words, why are you going to risk financial ruin, your marriage, your friends, your livelihood, legal prosecution, all to do this? You have to have strong motives and motivations—a why that is greater than just making money.

Research is another thing that we like to see. Researching is free. I shouldn't be able to google about your business and find out more than you know from the top three results. I want to be able to learn from whoever is sitting across the table.

Q: *Going back to the glassblower example, what else can the founder do to improve his or her odds of getting singled out for Gateway?*

A: First, I'd say, find a co-founder or two if you don't have any. Coming up with a prototype of your product or something that shows you will be able to execute also helps.

Q: *When looking at founders, do you ponder education, or do you consider every applicant?*

A: It is not as likely for us to fund and mentor a company founded by people straight out of high school. But if they had an incredible insight that no one else has, then we might. If they came out and said, for example, "This is a product that really speaks to the Generation Zers, and only I know that because I am the only Gen Zer in the room, plus I've been, say, baking cookies since I was 10 years old," then we might consider it as the kind of breakout that we need to take a risk on.

Q: *Now let's imagine someone who's pretty uneducated but has been working in the cannabis industry for a few years, learning the ins and outs of the trade. Would you support him or her?*

A: He or she could *become* a candidate. If this person approached me with a good insight, I would say, "Go execute on it."

If you come to me in 12 months and show me that you have used your experience from the industry to then turn around and do whatever it is that you want to do and that you've found a way to bootstrap it and be resourceful and just got something out there to the world—and can prove to me that people want it—we would consider you. We have certainly considered founders with nontraditional backgrounds before, but we make sure that they can succeed and eventually attract a few million dollars from venture capitalists.

We do encourage people to come to us. Even if they are not admitted in the program immediately, we will still help them, give them feedback, advice, and pitch practice for free. This was in fact the case of a company called Lumen, which makes hemp juices and is now in the program.

And here are some similar questions and the responses from CanopyBoulder's Micah Tapman:

Q: Would you look at founders without MIT graduate diplomas or Harvard MBAs? Would you consider funding a high school dropout?

A: I don't care too much about degrees. Of course, degrees make things easier; they open the door. . . . I get this from both sides because, as an investor, I recognize the value of, let's say, a Stanford degree. That will make it a lot easier for an entrepreneur to get a meeting with investors. On the other side, I dropped out of both high school and college.

My comment to people would be: starting a business is about skill—not about your resume. That's what makes entrepreneurship so much fun: the meritocracy. If you are really good at what you are doing, then you can get in the door. It might take you time, it may be harder if you don't have an Ivy League degree, but . . . I'm still going to talk to you because I don't even really look at resumes; I don't care.

Having said this, you have to know that dropping out of high school will likely make your life harder. I knew this and did it anyway, so tough luck for me. I made that decision and then took care of the consequences.

Q: So what do you look at then?

A: Before meeting with an entrepreneur, I will glance at his or her LinkedIn profile. I will take a meeting with him or her, talk with him or her for maybe 20 minutes, form an opinion about whether or not you have the chops to be involved in this at all, and then I'm going to do deeper due diligence if I think it's worth it.

After that, I will look at the team and see if you have a salesperson, a technology person, an operations person, a person with vision and big-picture understanding . . . It might be a small team, where each person does two or three things, or it could be a team of five people where each person has very specific tasks.

Q: What would you say to someone who argues that the cannabis industry has reached a level of professionalization where only highly educated people with a proven business or startup track record can succeed?

A: I think that it's possible to get involved in every industry. There is always room for people to help in a way and get involved. I'll say this again: entrepreneurship is about skill. So if you are skillful and you are good in an area, then you can usually make room for yourself.

Now another question is whether it is hard or easy to make room for yourself. Fortunately, in the cannabis industry, it is still very easy to make room for yourself and your company. Unlike the technology industry, cannabis is not hypercompetitive yet; you won't be up against 20 other companies including Google, Microsoft, and Apple.

In the end, Tapman suggests, the best thing you can do is build authentic relationships with investors and people in the industry.

▶ Paragon and the Canopy Experience

Sam Zartoshty is the co-founder of Paragon (http://joinparagon.us/), a CanopyBoulder graduate from one of the early cohorts.

Some of the participants in CanopyBoulder's acceleration program are already established, even generating revenue, he says when asked about his experience. Others, like Paragon, go into the program with "nothing more, and nothing less, than an idea."

There are a few things that any entrepreneur needs to understand when going through an incubation process, he explains. The first thing you have to know is what you want to get out of the program.

"I saw some people who really knew what they were doing, what they needed to learn, the connections they needed to make," he says. "Some other people (and I may have been one of them) had no idea what they were doing and just jumped in without doing any research on investing or accelerators before getting thrown into this whole boot camp.

"One of my main takeaways from Canopy was, in fact, that the people who knew what they wanted to get from the program were the ones who saw the most success," he adds.

▶ **Paragon and the Canopy Experience,** continued

Incubators are conceived to help, guide, and advise entrepreneurs. However, inexperienced entrepreneurs often find it harder to pick up and capitalize on everything that happens around them during the few weeks or months of the acceleration program.

One of the things Zartoshty *could* take advantage of was CanopyBoulder's strong network. Even if you don't know anyone in the cannabis industry when applying to CanopyBoulder—although you should—you'll finish your first day having met many of the space's leaders.

"Accelerators like CanopyBoulder, or Gateway in Oakland, or any of these other accelerators that I am sure will start popping up, have built strong connections, and they will share them with their companies from day one," he says. "They will give you their stamp of approval, and it's the best you can get: a smart investor's stamp of approval.

"The main thing I gained from Canopy was having that stamp of approval. Even for a guy like me, a young, inexperienced entrepreneur, getting that stamp of approval was enough to gain immediate respect from industry operators. And that is something that has held true for two years now," he adds. "When people hear somebody went through Canopy, they tend to ask for their contact information instead of brushing them off because they perceive you as someone who is successful or will be successful."

But there's more to an acceleration program than connections and a stamp of approval. They often educate investors in how to raise money and offer many other resources to help them build a network.

"I didn't even know what a pitch deck was before I went through Canopy. I thought that 'pitch deck' was a synonym for 'PowerPoint presentation,'" Zartoshty confesses.

"But isn't getting funded the whole point of applying to an incubator?" you may be asking.

It may come as a disappointment to know that the money these firms offer is rarely enough to start a business. As mentioned in Chapter 3 and in Marijuana Business Daily's Factbook, very few businesses can be set up with less than $100,000.

"What an accelerator will typically do is prepare you to have an amazing pitch and, when you're ready, provide an introduction to investors," Zartoshty explains, pointing out that accelerators are not only about financing. In fact, financing is, to many, the least important thing an accelerator can provide. Their value, they argue, lies in learning how to pitch investors outside the accelerator.

▶ **Paragon and the Canopy Experience,** continued

So here's another important lesson: make sure you really understand the scope of the program you are applying to.

"Entrepreneurs really need to do their due diligence on these different accelerators and ask the different companies that have gone through them about their experience because these people will be taking ownership in your company—and you shouldn't give away your company to someone you don't trust or who isn't going to add value to you," Zartoshty recommends. "It really blows my mind how few people have reached out to ask about my experience."

Zartoshty initially set out to build a social network, the "LinkedIn for cannabis," with job listings being just a free feature in it. He was pretty set on that concept. However, after dozens of people in the industry told him they did not need another social network, but instead a platform to find quality employees, he decided to modify his original concept.

And this is the last piece of advice Zartoshty shares: If you decide to go through an incubator, do it with an open mind. "They will tell you to take customer feedback and potentially pivot to what the customer wants. Even if it hurts, you have to be open to this," he says. "You have to be humble enough to understand that the idea that got you into an accelerator might not be the business that you end the program with, if you want to be successful."

"Beyond the industry connections, what's great about an accelerator program is the cohort you are in. Being surrounded by people with extremely high levels of professionalism and intelligence on a daily basis kind of forces you to boost your own level of professionalism," he concludes.

Crowdfunding Alternatives

Another financing option apart from family and friends, and institutional and high-net-worth financers, is the crowdfunding route—paved by the 2012 Jumpstart Our Business Startups Act, better known as the JOBS Act, a law that seeks to return capital formation to retail investors by relaxing some of the securities regulations in place. What this implies is that instead of getting a lot of money from one or a few investors or groups, you will get a little money from each of many smaller backers.

There are two main crowdfunding mechanisms in existence today: regular crowdfunding and initial coin offerings.

Regular Crowdfunding

In regular crowdfunding, businesses register on a crowdfunding platform and ask the general public for money in exchange for:

▶ *Material rewards like merchandise or a product.* You might be familiar with some platforms offering this service, like Kickstarter, Indiegogo, and GoFundMe.

▶ *Equity in the company.* Limits are put on the amount that can be raised vary depending on the crowdfunding categorization, ranging from $1 million to $50 million.

In the past, only accredited investors (people with at least $200,000 in annual income or a net worth of $1 million or more) could acquire equity in a company. But new SEC rules allow anyone to invest in crowdfunding campaigns. The amount, however, still depends on annual income and net worth.

On the one hand, these new rules have helped return capital formation to the general public, ending a cycle whereby only Wall Street investors could reap the benefits of getting aboard a business venture in its early stages. On the other, crowdfunding has allowed many companies to create unjustified hype and raise large amounts of money from uneducated investors without ever providing a clear business plan or path to profitability and ROI.

If you decide to take the crowdfunding path, you'll need to choose the right platform and develop a strategy to differentiate your pitch from the rest of the candidates'. A nice way to drive interest is to invest in marketing, public relations, and advertising, experts often suggest. We will share some tips on these topics and a list of people and firms doing this in Chapter 8.

In the meantime, you can start by doing some research on the options currently available for crowdfunding. Some crowdfunding platforms operating in the cannabis industry include:

▶ CannaFundr: www.cannafundr.com
▶ CrowdfundX: www.crowdfundx.io
▶ 420fundme: http://420fundme.com
▶ Fundanna: https://fundanna.com

CrowdfundX helps companies raise capital online. "We, on behalf of the client, market investment opportunities that live on platforms like the ones listed above," director of marketing Aaron Mendez explains.

"Separately, and more interestingly, we can actually set companies up to raise capital directly on their own website instead of on a platform. We call this an 'owned and operated campaign,' in which we market the issuer's offering (that lives on their own website) to our investor database as well as new potential investors."

Blue Cord Farms is one company that decided to raise capital through crowdfunding to support a project that will start with a caregiver storefront in Maine and evolve toward recreational sales when they become legal in that state. "The original thought was to expand the current operation into a large facility where we can hire vets and teach them to grow," Iraq veteran and CEO Robert Head says. "Our plan now is to open up one shop and create a small business that can expand to recreational once recreational sales are approved.

"We have also been in touch with the PTSD Foundation of America. The mission with them is to start a counseling session that involves cannabis for veterans close to our farm in Maine. My goal for this is to get these vets off the hard pills and make the switch to cannabis."

When asked why he decided on crowdfunding, Head explains, "I chose crowdfunding over any other forms of investor opportunity because we felt it was a faster way to raise funds."

As of March 4, 2018, and with 11 days to invest left, the company has managed to raise $12,450, or roughly three-quarters of the $20,000 it needs, from a total of 29 investors.

An even larger, established company that chose to walk the crowdfunding path is True Leaf Medicine International. Even though the company already trades in the Canadian Stock Exchange under the MJ symbol, and at the OTCQB under the TRLFF ticker, its management decided to raise additional capital from the public to fund its expansion via a Regulation A+ mini-IPO. In January 2018 the company announced the offering had raised $10 million.

"We saw Regulation A+ crowdfunding as not only a great way to increase our shareholder base but also potentially a way to drive sales and increase our brand awareness," CEO Darcy Bomford says. "The structure of the Reg A+ model allowed us to market the offering to our customers, all of them—distributors, retailers, and consumers included—and give them the ability to own a piece of the company they believe in. We set the minimum buy-in low (500 shares or $350 CAD) and offered 'perks' of free product and accessories based on the size of investment to incentivize participation.

"In our view, the whole world is going online, and this is the start of the same and a big paradigm shift for the capital markets," he adds. "Traditionally, companies such as us could only market to sophisticated or 'accredited' investors that met certain asset requirements. The Reg A+ model allows anyone to invest up to a maximum of 10 percent of their annual earnings, making it much easier to attract interest from a broader base of investors. Also key to maintaining a healthy public company share price is a wide shareholder base of investors who are motivated to go 'long' and hold the stock. Crowdfunding investors certainly fit that bill and help support the stock over the long run."

Pointing out how fascinating the Reg A+ experience was, Bomford recommends entrepreneurs "learn as much as they can before making the decision and look into all of the costs and time required to make it a success."

"It isn't easy, but the opportunity to attract a potentially huge and devoted shareholder base makes it worthwhile," he adds. So while crowdfunding might be an attractive option, it is also a complex one. You will need considerable advisory aid to conduct a compliant raise among the public. Ponder carefully whether this is the right option for you; if you decide it is, know there is no way around paying for professional help. If raising money for a cannabis business from accredited investors is complicated, raising it from the public is nothing short of an ordeal—as evidenced by Blue Cord Farms' difficulty to raise just $20,000.

Initial Coin Offerings

ICOs, or initial coin offerings, were one of the hottest financial topics of 2017. Put simply, an ICO (pronounced *I-see-oh*) is a fundraising mechanism whereby a company issues a virtual token, similar to (and often based on) Bitcoin, and sells it to the public under the promise that it will surge in value.

Each investor can buy as few or as many of these tokens as he or she pleases. But, unlike other crowdfunding mechanisms, he or she won't be acquiring an equity stake in the company.

It should also be noted that as of early-2018 ICOs are not regulated by the SEC—although some experts are working on a regulatory framework. This means there are few watchdogs out there making sure companies don't act maliciously, increasing the chances of fraud.

Again, there are many ICOs going on right now, so you might want to find ways to stand out among the crowd. A few things you can do, other than investing in marketing, public relations, and advertising are: hire a broker-dealer to issue your token, back it with some kind of security (instead of a utility function), and offer an easy way to convert the token into cash.

If all this sounds complex, that's because it is. You should therefore get advice from ICO experts, like Vincent Molinari and Christopher Pallotta of Templum, or the people at Medici Ventures, Overstock's blockchain-focused subsidiary.

Having said this, ICOs are rarely a good option for very young companies. In fact, many investors would never acquire a token that is not secured or backed by a company they know well. Others, however, motivated by the right marketing campaign, might take a leap of faith and invest in a new company via an ICO. This is the case of arguably the most notable (yet highly controversial) cannabis-related ICO to date: that of Paragon Coin, the blockchain project and underlying ICO led by beauty queen Jessica VerSteeg and backed by rapper The Game.

"With the right marketing campaign, you may get 5 percent of the people you reach to invest in your ICO," CannaSOS' Oleg Cheine shares based on his own experience. "In addition to spending a lot of money on marketing, you might want to get a famous person to support you. Otherwise, the media will not be interested in your project."

How to Attract Capital

Now that you know about all the different sources of capital available for cannabis businesses, what you need is a way to prove your business is a worthy investment. **Remember, a strong financial plan that takes into account one-time and recurring expenses, while outlining a path to returning money to your investors, is fundamental.**

Other important keys to getting investors interested are a one-page summary of your business and a PowerPoint presentation for people who liked the elevator pitch. Here's some friendly advice from iAnthus Capital Management's Hadley Ford: keep your presentation visual and no longer than 20 pages.

But what else do you need to exert a pull on capital?

After conducting a detailed analysis of the capital flow into the legal cannabis industry, Viridian Capital Advisors' president Scott Greiper and vice president Harrison Phillips have arrived at a seven-point checklist that any entrepreneur should consider when seeking to attract investors:

1. Compile a great management team and, if applicable, an outstanding board of directors.
2. Establish governance and financial controls.
3. Create real differentiation and a tangible road to generating return on investment for your supporters.
4. Have a strong, viable business model.
5. Create a clean capitalization structure and balance sheet.
6. Try to offer investors a liquid asset.
7. Focus your initial investor relations and public relations efforts on finding and reaching potential investors.

One final piece of advice: don't make promises you can't deliver on. Instead, tell your investors you will start small, make some money, return some capital to them, and basically, take things one step at a time.

Capital-Light Options

When discussing financing for cannabis businesses with experts and industry insiders, one frequent suggestion for those without easy access to capital is to come up with a capital-light business idea, meaning one that requires very little money to get going, like offering caregiver services or cooking homemade, cannabis-infused meals for paying customers.

While it's hard to raise money, many entrepreneurs argue that you can always work harder. The story of Jeff the 420 Chef, featured in the sidebar below, will clarify a lot of issues about capital-light businesses.

"I often read stories about entrepreneurs giving up on their dreams because they don't have enough resources—enough capital. But if you were to fail because you don't have enough capital, it's not because of that really. It's because you are not willing to put in enough time and effort into finding a solution to your problem," CannaSOS' Daniel Cheine says. "However, to achieve this, you have to be passionate about what you do. Without passion, you will most likely fail."

> ## ▶ Meet Jeff, the 420 Chef
>
> Few stories illustrate how one can build a business with little or no capital whatsoever better than that of Jeff Danzer, best known as Jeff the 420 Chef (www.jeffthe420chef.com).
>
> Jeff started making pot brownies a few years ago and has since been dubbed "The Julia Child of Weed." He built a brand out of his name, published a book, created a podcast, and started several other companies including The Cannabis Cooking Channel. Of course, the cannabis industry has changed substantially since Jeff got into it, but there are a few takeaways that are still very valid.
>
> "I think that, if you have something really unique and special that you do outside of the cannabis space and you can bring that into cannabis, then you'll find cannabis is an absolutely great place for an entrepreneur to start a business," Jeff says, reflecting on his trajectory. But you *do* have to have something special to stand out in the crowd.
>
> Back in 2012, Jeff was cooking for a friend of his mother's who had cancer. She had a prescription for medical cannabis but could not smoke it. This might not sound like a problem nowadays, but things weren't as easy as they are today, where you just go into a dispensary and get a bag of cannabis-infused gummy bears, a transdermal patch, a topical ointment, a tincture, a bar of chocolate, or a cookie. So Jeff was making marijuana-infused brownies for her.

▶ Meet Jeff, the 420 Chef, continued

"I had learned how to make pot brownies in college, so I made some for my mom's friend. And they were horrible, terrible, they had this really grassy taste and we did not know how to measure the potency," Jeff says. "But even though it didn't taste good and the potency was off, word got out that I was doing this."

As people found out about Jeff's weed-infused brownies and the number of orders increased, one customer pointed out that "the virgin sister" (or cannabis-free brownie) he included in every batch was delicious—unlike its medicinal sibling. So he set out to replicate that flavor in his cannabis-infused edibles. The big question was how to get rid of that plant taste.

After a year and a half of research, Jeff found out that the unpleasant taste "was not coming from the actual medicine on the plant, the trichomes, which are hydrophobic, meaning they stick to the plant and won't come off with water," but from the chlorophyll in the buds. So he decided to try washing the weed.

Experimenting with different cleaning methods, he arrived at a procedure that allowed him to "bleach the chlorophyll out of the plant" using distilled water and a blanching procedure: boiling and then quickly shocking the buds back to cold. At the end of this process, his weed was almost tasteless, and so were his cannabis-infused oils and butters.

Taking advantage of this discovery, Jeff started baking cannabis-infused cupcakes that were free of that grassy taste. A friend tasted them and suggested he reach out to a guy he knew, Justin Jones, who worked at The Daily Beast.

Having tasted Jeff's cupcakes, Jones came out with a story he titled "Meet the Julia Child of Weed." That article catapulted Jeff to fame, including a book deal and interest from TV producers.

Jeff believes the universe guided him along, giving him everything he needed to make it happen "because it needed to happen." However, there is more to this story than fate. Jeff's story proves the value of perseverance, the importance of having a good idea and a differentiated product, and the fact that one can start a successful business without millions of dollars, or even hundreds of thousands, in funding. "It's all about having something unique to offer," he reiterates.

So what does Jeff suggest aspiring cannabis chefs and potential culinary entrepreneurs do?

"If you look outside the cannabis industry, the culinary industry is one of the largest in the world, with all these chefs out there and all these restaurants out there," Jeff says, pointing out that, within the cannabis industry, the sector has not fully developed. Yes, there is an edibles industry but not a culinary industry—it's as if we had Nestlé and Kraft Foods but no restaurants.

To start a successful cannabis business, you need to figure out what you do "really, really well," he continues. "This is marketing 101: If you want to stand out, you need to offer something special, have a unique selling proposition."

His last piece of advice: "If you want to break into the cannabis business in a big way, you need to be seen—you need to be heard. So if you have any bit of money, or connections, or whatever, you need to get your product in front of the press; you need to get the product out there so that somebody can write an article about it. Get samples together, get out there, (and) meet with people who can spread the word for you because word of mouth is huge."

Finally, be sure to get informed about all the rules and regulations that apply to cannabis businesses. Be smart, find ways to legally do what you want to do, Jeff recommends. In some cases, you'll need to become certified as a caregiver to prepare cannabis-infused meals; in others, you can't provide your customers with cannabis, but you can cook for them using their own cannabis, and charge them for that service; in still others, you'll need to start a collective and have customers join it before you can serve them.

For more on Jeff's story, read the full exclusive article at http://entm.ag/36j.

Now that you are familiar with all the different funding options at your disposal, you can find the one (or combination) that is best suited for your business. It's crucial to know how much capital you need as well. Overcapitalization is one of the most prevalent problems among cannabis businesses. Raising too much money at the start will likely have you struggling with debt pretty soon.

Raising capital for a cannabis business is no piece of cake. While family and friends may be able to provide you with seed capital, building a strong business requires a lot of money. So you should consider the following options:

- Family offices
- Cannabis-focused investment funds
- Angel investors
- High-net-worth individuals

▶ Accelerators
▶ Crowdfunding

Also remember that most investors will want you to explain why your idea is special, your model is viable, and your business scalable. In addition, consider bringing in a partner who complements your abilities and knowledge and, again, always remain compliant!

6

The
Licensing
Issue

All businesses require a business license, although only those touching the plant, especially those growing or selling marijuana, need a cannabis-specific license on top of the regular one. In this chapter, you will find out which forms of licensing apply to you and your business so you can stay on the right side of the law.

Before you get started, remember that attention to detail is vital. In this line, make sure to have every document needed to apply for a cannabis license. Examples of things you may need include a proper business license, a registration with the secretary of state, workers' compensation insurance, etc.

So the first piece of advice is to work with a corporate attorney to properly license and register the actual business that is going to apply for a marijuana license.

"For all license types, at least in California, one of the basic requirements is to have some kind of business formation even if it's a sole proprietor," Amelia Hicks, Senior Environmental Scientist at California's Bureau of Cannabis Control, adds. "The business formation aspect is regulated by the secretary of state in California, and it's actually quite an easy and cheap process to register a business."

Once you've completed your business registration, you'll be ready to move on to your marijuana license application.

The Cannabis License

As with many other elements in this industry, the cannabis licensing process varies from state to state and even from municipality to municipality, so the first thing you'll need to do is get acquainted with your jurisdiction's rules, regulations, and requirements. To make things simple, though, let's divide the processes into competitive and noncompetitive processes.

States with competitive processes (like most of the East Coast states) will offer a limited number of licenses and require applicants to prove they are the best suitable candidates. Think of it as a government-style procurement process. This is how the application process works in states like Florida, Ohio, and New York.

Noncompetitive processes (usually found on the West Coast) tend to put no limits on the number of licenses that can be handed out; all that matters is that certain criteria are met. This is the case in Colorado, Washington, and Oregon.

Taking into account that the cost of a license and the thresholds to get one are usually lower in noncompetitive states, numerous industry insiders recommend you try and get your first cannabis business set up in one of these.

Let's take Oregon as an example. The application process there is done online. "There is a laundry list of things that you have to do; I wouldn't say it's grammar school–level stuff, but it's not that hard. It's more about just finding the right location and making sure that you respect water rights, in case you have any. But the licensing process is very state-specific," Green Light Law Group's Bradley Blommer explains.

In addition to getting professional help, become well-acquainted with your state's regulations. If you know the rules fairly well yourself, you won't have to run to your lawyer for answers to the easy questions and can save them for when the truly difficult problems come up.

tip

You can find a lot of state-specific information at http://norml.org/states.

"Just to get licensed, you will have to learn all of this. And in some cases, you'll need to learn other things like how to use the seed-to-sale system," Blommer continues.

Somewhere in between purely competitive states and noncompetitive ones, there are states like California where the process is not competitive on the state level but *does* become competitive on the local level—and local approval is necessary to get a license. In fact, the Bureau of Cannabis Control (one of the three cannabis business licensing agencies operating in that state) explains on its website, "Local jurisdictions may ban, in whole or in part, medicinal and adult-use commercial cannabis activity."

"The local authorization piece is probably one of the most challenging pieces. In California, we have 58 counties and 400 municipalities (cities or towns), and each of those local jurisdictions is authorized under the statutes to create its own rules and regulations for the cannabis business activity and can even ban these activities," Hicks explains.

Finally, states like Arizona demand dual licenses. For example, a marijuana grower must hold a cultivation license *and* a dispensary or retail license even if he decides not to get into retail.

Also fluctuating from state to state is the application window. Some states allow applications any time of the year, while others set application periods and deadlines maybe once a year. You will need to check with your state to find out their policy.

The Real Cost of a License

Licensing fees also diverge considerably. Some states charge an application fee of $250 and annual renewals of $1,000, while others ask for $25,000 to apply, another $200,000 if and when the license is granted, and a renewal fee of $100,000 each year. And those numbers fluctuate depending on the type of cannabis business you start.

Having said this, it should be noted that the cost of applying for a license is much higher than the fees the government charges. The application process will very likely require you to hire lawyers, accountants, consultants, and so on.

"In a state with a recreational program and a finite number of licenses, depending on the amount of consultants a business hires, the amount of effort they want to put in from a legal and lobbying perspective, and the money allocated to building a team, getting ready to apply for a license can cost anywhere between $200,000 and $2 million," iAnthus Capital Management's Hadley Ford estimates, adding it up on the back of an envelope. "In Florida, for example, people spend between $5 million and $10 million ahead of getting a license.

"So the license application process is not the same as it was five years ago, where you'd scratch together $20,000 from your savings account and mail your application," Ford adds.

Procuring a Cannabis License

Although each jurisdiction's cannabis business licensing process and requirements are unique, there are a few things most regulatory agencies want to see in applicants, Canna Advisors' Jay Czarkowski says. These are:

- ▶ A realistic, achievable, and "well-thought-out" business plan
- ▶ A sound financial model and the capital necessary to execute on it
- ▶ A strong, professional team—especially at the management level
- ▶ A plan that will not only generate money for you, your investors, the businesses that will interact with you, and state taxation agencies, but also bring benefits to the community in which it will operate, the state, and/or the patients
- ▶ A very detailed, long-term operational strategy
- ▶ A compliant physical location

Even though location was the last element on our list, it will often be the first one on regulators' lists. In almost every case, regulators will require your store or facility to be at a certain distance from schools, public parks, child-care centers, churches, libraries, rehab centers, community-service agencies, and other similar places. So make sure you have a compliant location secured before applying for a license.

Keep in mind that this applies to plant-touching businesses only. If you were to start, for example, a marketing business from home, you wouldn't need a cannabis license, although other business licenses might be required depending on your state's laws.

In addition to having a compliant location nailed down, you will need a letter from the landlord saying he or she is aware the space will be used for cannabis. This usually requires that the landlord owns the building and has no bank debt on it as well.

One last consideration in relation to choosing your location: never underestimate your electricity and water needs, and make sure the property's usage rights can cover them. People often undershoot on these requirements, Cura Cannabis Solutions' Cameron Forni says. "The infrastructure that's available and the cost of these resources are two other things that people often overlook," he adds. "These things end up setting businesses *years* behind."

On a personal level, regulators like to see that the person or people applying for a license are easily reachable through online profiles like LinkedIn, Hicks adds. "By making oneself available through networking platforms, I think information is more readily available.

"Beyond paying attention to what the rules and regulations are in your local jurisdiction, you should consider reaching out to the regulatory agencies and ask questions about the licensing process. This will predispose regulators better," she concludes.

A few good questions to ask are:

▶ What are the general, personal conditions I need to fulfill to apply for a license?
▶ Are there any limitations regarding who can and cannot apply for a license?
▶ Are there any water-usage or energy-usage limits or regulations?
▶ Are there any security aspects at my business's chosen location that need to be taken care of before applying for a license?
▶ What documentation do I need to get from my landlord?
▶ Which type of advice should I get? Do I need a lawyer? A CPA? A licensed architect?
▶ And finally, is there any way I can make regulators' jobs easier? How can I help them process my application more smoothly? How can I avoid placing any unnecessary burdens on them?

Surging Complexity

As the license application process becomes more complex, regulators want to see additional features in applicants. "You have to show expertise around not just cannabis but also banking, security, regulations. Getting a new license might sound like a pretty straightforward thing, but it's actually a complex process," iAnthus Capital Management's Hadley Ford says.

Going back to the advice he shared in Chapter 2, Ford notes that the best way to learn about licenses is to get a job at a licensed cannabis business just as the best way to learn a language is to move to a place where that language is spoken. "Within six months, you will know more about the business than you ever cared to know," he says, explaining that knowing how a cannabis business and the wider industry work can do a lot for an applicant in the eyes of regulators.

Applying for a license requires a lot of attention to detail. This includes being very careful about who your partners and team members are. Sometimes, having a person with a DUI in your team can be enough for you to get rejected.

One final tip: Don't volunteer information. Providing more information and legal documents than the regulatory agency requires can get you in trouble. There is such a thing as being "too compliant." Imagine, for instance, that you disclose the seed money for your cannabis business came from your mother; in the eyes of regulators, your mother is involved in your business, even if all she did was lend you money.

"Some licensing agencies are evaluating 120 applications at a time. So if you get them everything they want (not more, not less) as quickly as possible, you are going to get through the system with as little hardship and damage as possible," Anne Van Leynseele says. "As long as you are well-prepared as an applicant, follow the rules, and have the guidance of a CPA and a lawyer to decide what you should turn in and what you shouldn't, then you are going to get through the licensing process fairly quickly—because they want to get to 'yes' and get you off their desk."

"Additional information tends to convolute things," Amelia Hicks concurs, suggesting you submit only the required documentation and nothing more.

Product Licensing and Final Advice

In addition to the regular business license and the marijuana license, some businesses will need to apply for a product license. To qualify, you will likely need to show that your packaging is childproof and that you have fulfilled every labeling requirement.

Again, every state will want something different, so learn the rules before applying. A good first step is developing a relationship with the licensing body, and make sure you submit your packaging for approval prior to manufacturing thousands of units.

"A wrong number or even the presence of a colorful animal in your packaging can get you rejected," Cura Cannabis Solutions' Cameron Forni warns.

"One last thing you should consider is that being an early applicant usually increases your odds of getting a license," Forni ends. "The later you apply, the longer the line has become."

Another big mistake people often make is not being involved in the city or county where they are applying for a license. "Very often people get real estate in the hopes that a certain locality will allow for cannabis production [for example] without knowing how the people in the county will vote," Forni adds. "Many times, they end up not being able to apply for a license after the vote and get stuck with an expensive piece of real estate they will never be able to use for cannabis."

Also make sure that the area in which you want to set up your business is not an outlier or unincorporated county. In other words, make sure that not only the state but also the locality of your choice will allow you to operate a cannabis business.

▶ California Is for Cannabis

Before recreational cannabis legalization took effect in California in 2018, the state created a new categorization for "commercial cannabis activity" licenses. Each license covers a pretty specific activity.

Broadly speaking, there are six types of licenses:

1. Retailer

2. Retailer (nonstorefront)

3. Distributor

4. Distributor transport

5. Testing laboratory

6. Microbusiness (vertically integrated businesses, not necessarily small ones)

Check out which types of businesses are included in each category at the Bureau of Cannabis Control of California's site (https://cannabis.ca.gov/wp-content/uploads/sites/13/2017/03/17-191_ Information_Workshop_v3.pdf).

For California applicants without a lot of money or a clear business plan, the state is offering temporary licenses.

"Those license applications only require three pieces of information: we need to see that you have landowner approval (for example, a lease and some documentation that shows that your landowner knows a cannabis business will be operating there); a local authorization piece; and a premises diagram," the bureau's Amelia Hicks explains.

In fact, the bureau has launched an online licensing system to process applications for commercial cannabis licenses. You can access this system at http://online.bcc.ca.gov. Note that the processing of temporary license applications is not only prioritized but is also free of charge.

Cannabis businesses require all sorts of licenses. So before applying for a business license, a cannabis-specific license, or a product/packaging license, make sure you know every last requirement; you might only get one shot at it.

Also take into account that the cost of a license is much higher than the licensing fee. Remember there will be legal fees, advisory expenses, accounting costs, and so on. So make sure you have enough money lined up to fund the process. If you don't have sufficient funds, consider a temporary license where these are available.

Setting Up Shop

O nce you have all the necessary licenses and permits you need in your hands, your next step is to set up shop even if you are not setting up an actual retail store but an office, manufacturing facility, or grow operation instead. This is where the final countdown starts: T minus 5.

During this phase of your business, you'll have to get everything ready for your market debut. So in this chapter, we'll look into how to take on the tasks of:

- Building your team
- Naming and branding your company
- Crafting your story
- Getting your physical location ready for its debut
- Conducting a soft launch and getting feedback
- Correcting all the things that do not quite work out
- Dotting all your Is and crossing all your Ts
- Conducting the internal and third-party final audits

"If you think you have something worth building a company around, don't stop. Never stop. There is a lot of work that can be done without spending a cent. Rent, employees, swag . . . it all costs money. There is so much that can be done before going into such expenses," Gateway's Ben Larson says.

"Make sure you know where to find customers and how to talk to them; be sure that this is a product that is solving a problem or filling a need that customers have; do an extensive naming exercise, asking yourself if it's simple and repeatable, if you can own it or there are trademark issues—and never base it on which .com domains are available because you'll end up with a very stupid name."

In accordance with Ben Larson, CanopyBoulder's Micah Tapman recommends keeping fixed costs as small as possible. For instance, consider leasing things like equipment or property instead of buying them. Also beware of contract lengths, especially when renting real estate. Just a few months after launch, the space you picked originally could prove either too big or too small for you.

"At first, many landlords gouge cannabis entrepreneurs, charging them huge leases, and people just sign these enormous long-term leases because they don't have many other options," Green Light Law Group's Bradley Blommer adds. "The thing is that you cannot cancel a lease just like that, and if you do and the tenant then rents the property for less money, technically you'll be on the hook for that difference."

So keep your expenses variable and as low as possible because you have no idea how this business is going to grow. "It's better to grow slower than expected than to run out of money fast," Tapman says.

Think of it this way: if you were to book a hotel room online, it would be smarter to go for a midrange hotel and pay a few bucks extra for free cancelation. In other words, don't buy a pair of Jimmy Choo shoes for a five-year-old; she'll outgrow them before they get worn out.

► Meet Brendan Hill

Brendan Hill is the drummer of the Grammy-winning jam band Blues Traveler. Over his life, he's had the good fortune of sharing a stage with The Rolling Stones, releasing a platinum record, starting the Spin Doctors (the band behind one of the quintessential songs of the 1990s, "Two Princes"), and even smoking a joint with Marilyn Manson, the members of Metallica, and Neil Young.

In 2015, as if his life had not been interesting enough, the famed musician decided to go on yet another adventure: opening a cannabis dispensary. Less than three years into this venture, his store is generating annual sales of more than $4 million.

So what's the secret to setting up a successful store like Hill's Paper & Leaf?

The story of how Hill and his partner, Steve Kessler, decided to start Paper & Leaf is long and extremely interesting. However, we'll skip the initial planning phase and cut to the point of this chapter: how the pair started a successful shop with little outside help.

Some things you need to know before moving on: Paper & Leaf is situated in the state of Washington, where recreational cannabis was legalized in 2013. Zooming in on the map, you'll notice the store is located on Bainbridge Island, a little isle near Seattle with just 24,000 inhabitants.

You might wonder how they make millions off such a small population. Well, there are two keys to this. On one hand, more than 70 percent of Bainbridge Island's population had voted in favor of legalization, so there was a clear local interest in marijuana. On the other hand, Bainbridge becomes very crowded during the tourist season, and anyone can buy weed in Washington as long as they are at least 21 years old.

"Steve and I had very similar ideas of what we wanted from a cannabis store," Hill says. "I am a musician, so I had been around cannabis for a long time; cannabis had been, for years, a part of my culture—my creative process. Steve also had an artistic background, so he was no stranger to cannabis."

Feeling in sync, the newfound friends decided to apply for a license. At the time, however, many jurisdictions in Washington were using a lottery system to determine who would qualify for a marijuana retail license.

When the numbers for Bainbridge Island were drawn, Hill and Kessler's business came out third. But they did not lose hope. "It looked like the location was going to be the deciding factor because there were so few locations in Bainbridge that were far away from parks, schools, (and) nonprofit centers," Hill says. "Fortunately, we had a lease on a property that was compliant."

Nonetheless, the partners had to spend the following seven or eight months waiting for the other lottery winners to find locations before the local regulatory agency decided on who would get the license in the end. Finally, on Christmas Day, they met with the lottery winner and agreed that he would share his "Golden Ticket" and become a silent partner.

Since neither had ever opened a store before, they played it by ear, taking what they liked from other cannabis retailers and changing what they didn't. One of the things they wanted to change was how the product was displayed. "A lot of prerecreational stores, medical dispensaries, had counters and a salesperson behind it, and you were basically just handed a paper menu to pick cannabis from," Hill says. "Quite often, you'd get limited time with the salesperson or budtender, and had to pick quickly.

"We wanted to do something different. We wanted people to be able to come into our store and be able to have a discovery moment where they can walk around the shop, like in a bookstore or a wine boutique, and be able to actually see the product, a description of the strain and its properties—THC levels and terpenes, and get some sort of emotional connection, a moment where you go, 'Wow, that is a really well-trimmed, well-taken-care-of bud.'"

The pair had leased an empty warehouse, so the possibilities seemed infinite. "We decided to take advantage of this and create an open floor plan. What was unique, in our minds, was that we'd create this kind of art gallery feel," Hill says, bringing up another important tip you should take into account when setting up shop, especially a retail operation: create a unique experience.

Each grower had his or her own little display box on the walls of Paper & Leaf, so they could all develop unique identities. In retrospect, this also seems like a pretty important factor in the dispensary's success: creating synergies with industry colleagues and providers generated incentives for everyone to constantly try to improve, enhancing all the products involved in the cycle.

As word of Paper & Leaf got out, an increasing number of growers started getting interested in selling their product there. It was like a virtuous circle where only the best growers would be admitted, making Paper & Leaf one of the best dispensaries in the state—something reflected in their online ratings.

▶ **Meet Brendan Hill,** continued

It's important to know how much money you have and spend it wisely, Hill concludes. "We were smart about doing a lot of the construction and design ourselves, so we had some money left to pay employees and reinvest in the business."

To get the full scoop on Hill's story, complete with exclusive quotes, head over to http://entm. ag/06j.

In fact, this goes beyond real estate. In general, never spend money if you don't need to. Your hands won't fall off if they get dirty, so don't pay someone to clean your place at first; do it yourself.

"It's also about psychology," Tapman adds. "It's subtle, but you end up creating an opportunity to think and reflect about what you are doing. It's almost like a meditation space or, if you do it with someone else, a time to get one-on-one time with your employees or partners to chat."

Before moving on to the prescriptions for this stage of your business buildout, take another look at the sidebar starting on page that brings Chapters 5 and 6 together.

T Minus 5: Building Your Team

Any company setting up shop must see human resources as its main priority. This is something that a lot of people overlook, and it ends up costing them a lot of money later on. So before taking any other steps, figure out what your HR structure will look like: who will be in charge? How will new employees be brought on board and embedded into your company? How will you handle things like discrimination, sexual harassment, and other policy issues?

"A company is just an organization of people that are united around a common mission, vision, and set of values," HERB's Matt Gray says. "A lot of people screw up because they hire the wrong people. So it's absolutely essential that you refine your hiring process and bring on well-cut people. This is the only way you'll get to fulfill your vision: by surrounding yourself with people who are smarter than you are. And that starts with the hiring process."

"Don't be afraid to bring in people who have more experience than you," Michael Gorenstein, the 31-year-old CEO of the Cronos Group, one of the largest cannabis companies in the world, agrees. "Experience matters."

However, the hiring process in the cannabis industry is extra hard. "Everyone focuses on the missing piece of capital, but because there is not a lot of capital around, you don't have a lot of people either, [especially at the middle management level]," iAnthus Capital Holdings' Hadley Ford says. "You don't see people flocking into the cannabis industry as you see people flocking into the next hot tech area or the next hot investing area."

Beyond the relative lack of capital, one of the main reasons behind the scarcity of experienced people is the industry's young age. Imagine, for instance, that you are looking for a regional manager for your cannabis company. Where would you find someone with five or eight years of experience? There aren't a lot of people with such a background.

"You can find someone who knows how to grow, and you can find someone who wants to be your CFO, but things get very tricky at the middle management level," Ford concludes.

So how should you take on the hiring process? One of the main things you should consider is structuring your selection process around your mission and vision. You will want to question people on the topics related to your core values, Matt Gray suggests, mentioning that at his company, the focus is on finding "customer-obsessed" employees.

"Never settle in this arena," he says. "There will be a lot of noise and a lot of people that say they can do something, but they can't."

Canna Advisors' Tyler Stratford has extensive experience in this field, having played a central role in opening some of the first cannabis businesses in Alaska, Florida, Illinois, Maryland, Minnesota, and Nevada. In his opinion, a personnel selection process should start with upper management and then move down the hierarchy ladder.

Make sure to cross-train your employees, though. This generates all sorts of benefits. In fact, giving employees a clear idea of how growth within your company looks will help you reduce the elevated turnover that most cannabis businesses experience, Stratford assures. Remember, training employees does not just consist of teaching them their everyday tasks but also how to respond to emergency situations and other unexpected problems. All vertical businesses on the cannabis scale vary in the type of employees on staff and what that means for the level of training and hours worked.

A way to test people after the interview phase is to set a 30-, 60-, or 90-day challenge. Set unique milestones that you want your new employees to hit, and check back consistently to measure their performance and see how you can train them better. For instance, if it's a salesperson you're bringing onboard, set a 90-day sales target, and ask her to come up with a written plan to make this happen.

During the team buildup and training phase, you should also select the software products you will use and start teaching your employees how to operate them. Software will not only make your job easier and your operation more efficient and profitable, but it will also help you remain compliant. In fact, try to find products that integrate well with your state's tracking systems to remain on the safe side.

To recap, here are the main things to pay attention to when hiring personnel:

▶ Make sure the potential employees understand your mission and vision and can align with it.

▶ Start with upper management, then move down to middle management, and so on.

▶ Have a training program in place that includes some cross-training.

▶ Set objectives that your new hires should hit within 30 to 90 days of coming onboard.

T Minus 4: Branding Yourself

Until a few years ago, most cannabis brands were not especially sophisticated. However, this is no longer the case. If you've ever seen legal cannabis products in a store, you must have noticed how cool, modern, and beautiful they look. Of course, this is the result of an extensive creative branding process.

"One thing I noticed from the latest cannabis conventions and events is that the branders are finally starting to arrive at cannabis; the quality of trade show materials, logos, packaging, the positioning of these companies is *unbelievable*. As things continue to evolve, you can tell there is a lot more careful and professional consideration going into how these brands are positioned and communicated," Civilized's Derek Riedle points out.

"In such a stigmatized industry, it's very important to have very clean branding and marketing material," Avicanna's Aras Azadian adds.

You will likely need professional help to do this the right way unless you are *really* good at branding and communications. When selecting a professional or team to provide you with this service, pay attention to how many questions they ask. If some of these questions make you uncomfortable, that's even better. If they aren't asking any, it is very likely they are more interested in designing something *they* like than in creating the best branding concept for your company.

"I think that one of the hardest things for people to wrap their heads around is that branding *isn't* a logo. The logo is like the execution of the brand, but the brand is basically the thought or feeling you want people to have when they think about your product or your name," JJ Kaye, co-founder of design consulting firm High Pressure Zone, says. "Most customers in the cannabis industry will not have a deep knowledge of the qualitative difference between brands. So the way to differentiate yourself is to craft a strong story around your brand and show the consumer how your product is going to fit into his or her life.

"Bad branding is just yelling at the customer: look at me, look at me! Good branding, instead, is a little more patient; it creates curiosity and invites people to explore more and understand more."

Below is a list of the top priorities when you create a brand, regardless of what you sell:

► A strong, compelling story
► A name that resonates with your target customers
► A name that you can trademark on a federal level and that will help you get strong search results
► A logo, along with variations (e.g., black and white, single-color, reverse-color for dark backgrounds, etc.)
► A color palette to use in every branded product
► A type/font that will identify your brand
► A website and social media profiles

More often than not, your end consumer will not be anything like you, so you need to accept that your brand will be for your customers—not for you. "Don't just think about what *you* like (and) what *you* buy. Think about the end consumer's preferences, about what they value, about what they are going to buy, and craft an aesthetic, tone, and narrative that resonate with them," Kaye adds.

"A lot of entrepreneurs in the cannabis industry believe they are representative of their customers. That has created a scenario where many businesses market to themselves—to the user base that already exists in cannabis; everybody is going after the same type of consumer," John Sidline, principal at The Cannabis Story Lab, says.

But while positioning is key, it won't allow you to capture the entire cannabis market with your product. "The growth of cannabis and size of this industry is going to be mammoth, ultimately outpacing the beer and wine industries. So don't think you can eat the entire elephant," Riedle agrees.

But what can you do to get the biggest slice possible?

Crafting Your Story

The cannabis business is all about storytelling. This doesn't mean that you have to be able to weave a good tale around the campfire; rather, it means you need to tell your cannabis story in a way that shows customers and investors you are personally invested in your product or service. A good story goes a long way toward building goodwill and relationships that will help your business over the long run. Take the advice of Jared Mirsky, the founder and CEO of Wick & Mortar—formerly known as Online Marijuana Design, one of the top cannabis branding agencies out there, and winner of Best Branding Agency at the 2017 DOPE Industry Awards. More than a decade of experience in this field has led him to the conclusion that crafting a strong story for your brand is the best first step you can take toward strong branding.

"What most business owners do not realize is that when going through the branding process, there are little micro steps that need to be taken in order to ensure that the message and tone of the brand moving forward really make the most sense," he says.

Often, business owners base their name and identity on what they've seen or heard before, Mirsky explains. "But consumers need a real voice—not an echo. If you want to thrive in the cannabis industry, you can't be a copycat; there are just, quite frankly, too many. I mean, [there are so many companies named] Canna-this, Canna-that, Ganja-this, Ganja-that, Kush-this, Kush-that . . ."

We get it: your company is all about marijuana. But that doesn't mean your name has to include the actual product you offer. You don't see Apple calling itself Steve's Phones & Tablets, or Google changing its name to Alphabet Internet Services. The same applies to cannabis businesses: The most successful companies have easily identifiable names like Eaze, MassRoots, Leafly, Aphria, Organigram, Copperstate Farms, iAnthus, etc.

This connects to what Mirsky sees as step two in the branding process: creating the brand's personality. "There is nothing worse than having a bipolar brand," one without a clearly established personality, he says. It's all about cohesion and consistency in your image.

A Good Story

Regardless of the kind of attention you want for your brand, there's something you should keep in mind: the "cure for cancer" analogy. Spoiler alert: you're not really going to cure cancer. But take a look at Figure 7–1 on page 122 to see how you can find that big story that directly connects your business to a greater good; you just need to combine emotion and human benefit.

According to the "cure for cancer" theory, there are two main elements that make a story compelling: the level of benefit it can generate for humanity and the level of emotion it can create among readers. So on the lower left of this continuum is the humble screwdriver, which is only mildly useful and won't get anyone excited. "At the high end of the horizontal axis, you have low utility but high emotion—so something like professional sports, where it doesn't really serve a major function," John Sidline explains.

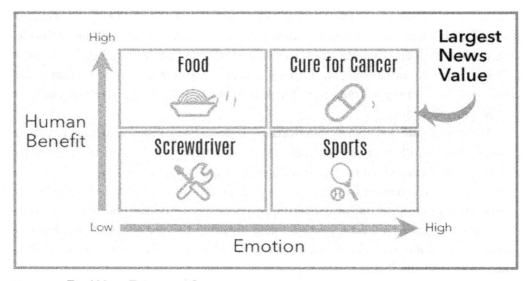

FIGURE 7–1: **Find Your Business Story**
Source: The Cannabis Story Lab. Find it at http://thecannabisstorylab.com/2017/10/10/narrative-vs-news.

At the upper left is food, which is highly useful, but still doesn't arouse wild excitement in most people (except for foodies). But on the upper right, we have the cure for cancer: something with high utility *and* high emotion. "In the noncannabis world, that's the Holy Grail," Sidline points out. "If you can find something that is akin to a cure for cancer, you can get stories all day long."

Nonetheless, in the cannabis world, that's the starting point. "Everybody in this industry begins there because everybody we've spoken to has a story where either cannabis helped them medically or it helped a friend medically," Sidline says. "And those claims don't necessarily have the kind of clinical backing to prove them, but that's the starting point."

Consequently, crafting a good story in the cannabis industry is even harder than normal. So allocate some time to finding the right combination of utility and emotion. This will be crucial to your future success. "And if this is a labor of love for you, make sure that comes through in your story," Sidline concludes. "If you believe in your product, other people will find it easier to believe in it as well. Enthusiasm is contagious."

Naming

Now it's time to choose a name for your business. As we mentioned earlier, pick a name that really reflects what you do without making it too self-explanatory. And never limit yourself to only those names with .com domains available! More likely than not, the .com domain for a good name will already be taken. Eaze.com, one of the top cannabis delivery platforms, did not start with that domain; it purchased it from the original owner when it could afford to do so.

The cannabis industry is still nascent, so a lot of potential customers don't really know what they are looking for.

"Most people will begin looking online with searches, so branding a product becomes really important," The Cannabis Story Lab's John Sidline says, recommending brands stay away from difficult-to-remember names, especially those combining letters and numbers to reference some detail in the product that only experts know about. "Don't be overly clever with your branding names because that's going to cause confusion or at least limit your ability to be discovered."

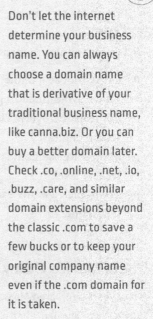

tip

Don't let the internet determine your business name. You can always choose a domain name that is derivative of your traditional business name, like canna.biz. Or you can buy a better domain later. Check .co, .online, .net, .io, .buzz, .care, and similar domain extensions beyond the classic .com to save a few bucks or to keep your original company name even if the .com domain for it is taken.

During the naming process, take into account trademark laws as well. Many cannabis companies nowadays are only registering in their own states without having looked at what companies are doing in other states. As a result, they spend a lot of money developing a brand that won't enjoy any trademark protection outside their state.

As an example, cannabis attorney Anne Van Leynseele tells the story of a client who didn't bother to register his trademark. His business grew and became successful. At one point, two employees left the company and started a similar business under the same name. Since the name was not registered, they got the trademark for themselves. The original business ended up spending $78,000 in legal fees over two and a half years to win back their own trademark when they could have prevented the problem entirely by just spending $3,000 registering their trademark when they set up the business.

"We recommend people registering their trademark on a federal level," Van Leynseele says. "We have found a way to do this quite easily."

One final consideration in naming is related to timing. While many industry insiders argue that picking a name for your brand should come after you've procured capital and permits, others believe this is one of the first steps you should take when conceiving a new business.

"Oftentimes, people choose a name because they need to throw something in their application without going through a formal branding process. But they don't realize how difficult it is to change that name once you've applied for many different things," Mirsky says.

So, to recapitulate, when choosing a name for your company:

▶ Don't choose a name based on which .com domains are available.

▶ Try to avoid including prefixes/suffixes like "canna-" and "mari-."

▶ But don't be overly clever either; remember people have to be able to find you on search engines.

▶ Make sure the name is not already trademarked and that you can register it on the federal level.

▶ Try to pick a name early so that every registration and legal document you file uses that name.

▶ Uncle Mark's Story

A few years ago, Jared Mirsky and his team had a client come to them with the name Uncle Mark's Farm. The name had a very special significance for the company's co-founders as it paid tribute to their actual Uncle Mark, a man in Oregon who had cultivated cannabis for medical users and ended up going to jail for it. During his time in the joint—no pun intended—Mark contracted hepatitis and eventually passed away.

As you might expect, Mirsky was moved by the story. However, he did not feel the company's name properly expressed this emotion, nor did it create "any intrigue or curiosity."

"When you think about the name 'Uncle Mark's Farm,' it seems pretty plain," he says. "In fact, it looks like every other company's name that has the word 'farm' at the end of it. There was nothing that I felt would really resonate with consumers."

Consequently, the Wick & Mortar team came up with a list of reasons the clients should consider changing the name. After an extensive naming exercise, they arrived at Rebel Spirit, a name they thought honored Uncle Mark's memory while also providing the company with the ability to connect with consumers and expand easily.

"Cannabis users tend to have a little bit of a rebel in them," Mirsky points out.

A Strong Identity

At the young age of 24, Matt Gray founded a media company that would become a multimillion-dollar business in just a couple of years. HERB is the most popular cannabis community on Earth and drives social media engagement levels on a par with Buzzfeed and Vice. In his opinion, the most important element in creating a strong, valuable brand is knowing your customer.

"Everything else kind of flows from that. But knowing your customer is essential, especially when figuring out how to talk to your customer," he says. "You need to survey your customers, ask the right questions, find out what are their struggles, how often they consume cannabis, how do they define themselves . . ."

Before going all out on a brand identity and a marketing message, you need to know whom you will be building your business for. "We have done this at HERB from the very beginning," Gray says. "We constantly scan the comments on our website and Facebook page to understand who these people are: where they are from, how old they are, how often they consume cannabis, etc."

This data is then used to craft HERB's content and video strategy. "Before we started making a bunch of videos, we wanted to know what our customers were looking for. No matter who you are, it's important to build a customer-obsessed company culture and one where you ask the right questions to your customer and then let them inform your strategy."

But how do you get that kind of data when you're not a polling expert?

Ask the right questions to the right people, without leading them on, Gateway's Ben Larson suggests. "And, please, don't go to your mom and your friends and ask them if they like your product because they are most likely going to say they do even if they don't."

Actually, finding people who *don't* like your product is very useful. Ask them why they don't like what you do, inquire about ways to get better, ask them about other people doing a better job at it—if there are any.

"Don't become complacent. This industry is changing really fast, so you have to stay on top," Larson adds. The data alone will not tell you all you need to know; for instance, a surge in demand for concentrates or edibles will not necessarily translate into a business opportunity for you if, for example, there are others who can make these products at a lower cost or sell them at more locations or get more shelf-space at dispensaries. Other times, the information doesn't mean what it appears to mean at first. This rise in demand for edibles and concentrates might actually be a reflection of an increasing desire among the public to find discreet ways to consume cannabis—meaning you could capitalize on this need in many other ways.

Graphic Aspects

After coming up with a solid name and conceptually clear brand identity, you should move on to developing a logo and other visual components of your brand, like the colors you'll use.

Keep in mind you cannot just grab an image from Shutterstock.com, change the colors, and make it your logo not only because it will probably look bad but also because it is usually not legal. "You can use something like 35 percent of an image, but you cannot pull an icon and just make it your company's logo," Mirsky explains. "If you do this, you'll end up dumping a lot of money into promoting a logo that, sooner or later, you won't be able to continue to use. It's almost like flushing money down the toilet."

> **tip**
> Steer clear of going green with your logo. It's an obvious, overused choice in the cannabis world.

So plan on paying for a good, custom logo that makes your company stand out from the rest. For instance, consider a color other than green as your main choice. There are so many cannabis brands using green logos today that customers often struggle to tell them apart.

As with so many elements in this industry, your branding process will be largely dependent on the type of product or service you will offer. Some companies might need a website from day one; others might be able to get by without one for the first few months. Some will need product photography; others won't. Some will need a strong social media strategy to build their brand; sometimes this won't be necessary. Some will need a sales collateral piece—a guide with the basics that anyone selling or distributing their product has to know; others won't need to worry about it.

Knowing who your customer is will be crucial in deciding these things because your graphic representation works like a calling card with your customer base. You'll eventually need a graphic approach for the following:

- ▶ Website
- ▶ Packaging
- ▶ Social media channels
- ▶ Print collateral
- ▶ Direct mail or marketing pieces

"By the time you debut, you want your website to be excellent and your social media to be on point; you want everything to look good, unique, and different from everything else that is out there," Celeste Miranda, founder and CEO at The Cannabis Marketing Lab, says.

As with many other aspects of starting a cannabis business, you might want a pro to help you create a graphic plan for your branding. The people at Wick & Mortar shared their complete pricing guide with us, so you could see how much it would cost to hire an award-winning creative agency to take care of your branding needs. They divide the process into three phases. Take a look at Figure 7–2 on page 128 for a breakdown of the typical costs associated with hiring a creative branding team.

B2B Branding

As you might anticipate, the branding needs of business-to-customer brands differ widely from those of business-to-business brands. So how should you go about starting a B2B brand?

"Business owners look at two things when they buy services from someone," High Pressure Zone's JJ Kaye explains. The first is how much the services cost and whether they are worth the expense. The second is whether the company they are hiring can actually deliver on its promises.

It's not that you won't need branding at all. However, most of your clients will judge your brand based on their experience with the salesperson they deal with or on a trusted person's recommendation. "B2B brands are much more sales driven. So salespeople have to really embody the brand and properly tell your story," Kaye says. "It's a more abstract version of branding."

Having said that, he clarifies that "there still is a certain degree of showmanship and sex appeal. So I wouldn't discount having a compelling visual identity, but it will need to be much more straightforward, literal, and to the point than a consumer brand where you can tell a broader story."

Design on a Budget

Knowing what full-blown branding and marketing services cost, you might decide to come up with the basics of your brand's identity on your own. While you should probably trust a pro with your design, sometimes budget constraints mean you need to prioritize spending. And you should always prioritize compliance services over other expenses.

The Cost of Creative Services

Phase 1: Identity

For a fee between $20,000 and $30,500, depending on how many of these services you request, you'll get:

1. A creative brief with the team

2. A brand mood board with a few variants

3. A few naming options

4. Logo design and a few alternatives

5. Stationery and social media graphics

6. A brand strategy and copywriting package

Phase 2: Packaging Design (And a Production Option)

For a fee between $17,000 and $25,800, depending on the number of applications you need for these designs, you'll get:

1. A creative brief with the team

2. A packaging mood board

3. Packing conception

4. Mockup applications

5. Technical applications

Phase 3: Website Design

For a fee between $5,000 and $25,000, depending on whether you choose to make a one-page site, a multipage site, or an ecommerce site, you'll get:

1. A creative brief with the team

2. One to three website concepts

3. One to five mockup applications

4. Website development

5. Ecommerce functionality, if applicable

6. Website presentation and revisions, if needed

7. Website transfer to a hosting platform of your choice and use tutorial

See the full detailed documents at this link: https://drive.google.com/open?id=1h_C-olToMzqOE214znkveSyD-CT-44KX.

FIGURE 7–2: **The Cost of Creative Services**

You will likely be able to come up with the conceptual basis of your brand without outside assistance, but you will probably need help with the more complex visual aspects of it.

"It's important to get a graphic designer who's motivated and wants to be involved in the industry and your business," Avicanna's Aras Azadian says; his company has a part-time, in-house design and marketing team.

Here are some pointers from Felipe Nosiglia, an architect turned cannabis brands designer, to help you learn what you need to know before going to an independent designer or graphic design studio.

The first thing Nosiglia asks his clients is for a filter of some kind. A PowerPoint presentation or PDF document of three to five pages introducing the brand's target audience and the way they want to position the product is enough.

"I sometimes get a few references and logos from other companies along with a comment down the lines of, 'Do something similar to this, add a little pink (since this brand is mainly for women), and we're good,'" he says. "But I can't work with such a vague concept. There are 100 ducks flying; I need to know which ones to shoot. I can shoot one, two, three, but not all of them."

His point is that every brand needs to clearly decide what its customer cluster is. "How old are they? What is their purchasing power? Are they forward-thinking or more conservative?" Nosiglia asks.

Also included in the brief "filter" document mentioned above should be a few words you think define your brand. Is it universal? Clean? Slick? Feminine? Cool?

"My job, same as an architect's, is to take these concepts and materialize them into a logo, typographies, a color palette, etc.," Nosiglia explains. "This is design 101, I know, but it's important. Each type, each color, touches a certain nerve in the customer, generates a certain emotion or feeling."

One thing to take into account during the design process is positioning, he continues. There are three common problems in this arena:

▶ *Overpositioning*, which makes customers believe your product is more expensive or less accessible than it really is. This drives many of them away because they believe they can't afford it or are not willing to pay an inflated price for it.

▶ *Underpositioning*, which is the opposite of overpositioning. This means your brand looks cheaper than it actually is, making your target customer uninterested in your products and those who find it interesting often unable to afford it.

▶ *Blurred positioning*, which means the consumer has trouble determining what kind of brand yours is. "This usually happens when the target customer cluster is too ample," Nosiglia says, as he explains that people should know a product is "for them," and not just for "anyone."

"In a general sense, there's too much focus on being a 'premium' brand," Eric Layland, founder and principal of cannabis marketing and branding firm Canna Ventures, says about brand positioning. Almost every entrepreneur who comes to his firm wants to be on the top tier. But "there's only so much room on the top shelf and not everyone can be there—nor should everyone be there," he says. "The market opportunity covers the full spectrum of mass-produced, high-volume [products] to artisan-crafted products."

Also important in the design process is knowing whether your brand aims at the mainstream or at a market niche. "People tend to think that going mainstream is better because you can catch more customers, but this is not always the case," Nosiglia explains, adding that your strategy will determine who you will target with your design—every possible customer, a few groups, or even just influencers and thought leaders alone as they can then generate a sort of spillover effect.

You should ask which strategy will be cheaper and/or have the greatest impact, he suggests. You won't always be able to shoot for all your target clusters, so you have to think strategically to better allocate your resources.

"We are hands on. Instead of outsourcing tasks, we are the ones out there talking to the consumer, we are the ones that have a feel for all of it, so that it's easy for us to brainstorm and directly work with a designer like Felipe, who is now a permanent member of our team," Avicanna's Azadian concludes.

T Minus 3: Getting Your Physical Location Ready for Business

This step will depend almost entirely on what line of business you'll be in. One thing that applies to any cannabis business, though, is this: you need to remain compliant at all times, have all the necessary security measures in place, and keep your place of business as clean and professional-looking as possible.

Also, pay close attention to things like security systems and the overall feel of the space, building, and neighborhood. As a rule of thumb, the more time you can spend conducting research and finding inspiration, the better the result will be. Beyond the real world, use the internet: look for ideas on Pinterest, Instagram, design sites, and company profiles on Leafly.com and Weedmaps.com.

If you go with a storefront or other public location, as opposed to operating out of an existing space or home office, be prepared for the challenges that come with prepping a new space, such as delays, permit issues, and code questions. Before starting Canna Advisors, Jay Czarkowski, a general contractor; Diane Stratford Czarkowski, a real estate agent; and Tyler Stratford, who came from a military background, were fixing and flipping houses. One thing they experienced *every* time was a delay in the construction process. "During construction, there are a lot of moving pieces; a lot of certifications you have to get along the way like plumbing, fire code, and occupancy," Stratford points out. "So be prepared for unforeseen delays (and) for not being able to avoid the unexpected."

> **tip** ⓘ
>
> If your budget allows for it, hire an architect or design expert; this will probably result in a much more efficient location. If you can't afford a professional, visit similar businesses and find inspiration there.

Just take it easy, don't get stressed, and realize it's all part of the drill. "It's a known evil that everyone faces," he says.

Stratford also says that getting your location ready for your debut is also about putting all the necessary infrastructure in place. "This ranges from hiring the employees that are not cannabis-industry folks (like your cleaning crew) to setting up your security system—not just your physical cameras but all the digital platform your security will run on," he explains.

"Anybody in a regulated market will have to interact with the state system and, on occasion, a seed-to-sale tracking system," he adds. "These are all things that have some effect on the physical layout of your location. They will have a lot to do with the flow of your business as you get it set up."

In other words, while you put your walls up, don't pay attention just to what's visible but also to what's inside them: wiring, plumbing, etc. Make certain all the pieces of your location work cohesively with one another.

If customers will be walking in, base your store or office's aspect on your branding strategy; clients will want to see synchronicity between them.

If you look at vertically integrated operations, for example, you'll see one branding approach across the whole line—a common feel. "Even if it's the offices or administrative areas, you want to create a safe, welcoming environment," Stratford says. "Figure out how to translate your brand to the physical aspect—not just taking the logo and mimicking it on wallpaper and business cards, but decide the general feel you will go for."

If it's a grow operation, make sure to get professional help to handle all things related to compliance with the law, from energy connections to water disposal. These regulations are complex and often not very lenient.

One final piece of advice: come up with some marketing material for your physical location. Even if it's just a small pamphlet, make it available to everyone walking into your space.

"Even if I just walk into your office for five minutes, I want to be able to walk away with something like a little foldout, trifold pamphlet of who you are, what you do, and how I can get ahold of you," Stratford concludes.

T Minus 2: The Soft Launch

Before your store officially opens, you should try out your security system and your point-of-sale system, create test entries taking advantage of the software products' sandbox features (making sure to erase that fake data before your market debut), and perform other trial runs. In other words, build in time to test all your systems and procedures in a soft-launch format before opening your doors to the public. According to Marijuana Business Daily, the two biggest challenges cannabis businesses without access to banking face are safeguarding cash and paying employees and vendors. Being prepared for them can save you massive headaches in the future. Once you've test-driven all the elements in your location individually, invite your family, friends, and colleagues to your shop, office, grow operation, or manufacturing facility and see what they think. Conduct this exercise at least once; if possible, spend two or three days at it. Ask people who will be candid about their opinions; it is likely your mother or best friend will not want to tell you if they don't like something—or might not even know what a cannabis-related business should look like.

"Don't just trust every person that gives you anecdotal feedback," Tyler Stratford says. "Prepare an actual questionnaire, highlight areas of concern which are confined . . . and get the customers to describe the general feel they get from your location. Did they feel rushed? Did they feel like the employees did not know what they were talking about? Those are some general things that stem from inexperience."

In addition to getting people's comments, take notes during the soft launch yourself. This will probably be the

> **tip** ⓘ
> Remember to only distribute cannabis products to people who can consume them legally in a place that is authorized to do so. In some ways, it's an even better idea to replace the cannabis products during your soft launch with something like candy just to see how people interact with your space rather than the product per se.

only time you'll be able to watch what's going on in your business; once you open you'll be too busy running the place.

In many ways, how people experience your brand is related to the tangible aspects of it, whether it's the physical location, the product, or even the people representing the brand. It's important to keep this in mind as you assess the results of your soft launch. What worked? What fell flat? What sort of branding outreach can you derive from what you saw during the soft launch?

"Especially with a product that customers will hold in their hands and consume, the tactility of it is very important," High Pressure Zone's JJ Kaye notes. "So, for instance, if you decide to place a demo of your product at a certain dispensary [or host a demo of a product in your store], don't just throw them together half-ass. You need to put your best foot forward; that's one of the very first touch points. The person doing the demo and educating people about the brand is basically representing your brand.

"Not thinking about that is really a missed opportunity to really create a connection and develop a lifelong consumer," Kaye adds, pointing to the importance that large retail chains like Neiman Marcus or Barneys place on creating a consistent brand experience.

Here's a checklist of a few things you should test during the soft launch:

▶ Your security system
▶ Your point-of-sale system
▶ Your location's general feel
▶ The way traffic flows inside the location
▶ How the product looks in your store, if applicable
▶ How the employees treat customers
▶ How customers react to interacting with employees
▶ How your staff reacts to unexpected scenarios
▶ How your staff manages an emergency drill

One final suggestion for the soft-launch phase from Tyler Stratford: "Throw in an issue. Have a scenario where somebody pretending to be drunk comes in, or come up with some kind of situation everyone in your team has to react to."

T Minus 1: The Final Audits

By this stage in the business buildout, you will very likely be tired. But don't put your head down just yet. There is one last step, and there is no way around it: the final audits.

▶ Does Your Grower Pass the Test?

Wick & Mortar has come up with "The Buyers Guide for Retailers and Dispensaries," a document with 28 questions to ask a grower to determine whether it's a good partner for your business. The report goes into each topic in detail; here are the basic questions:

1. Are they legally licensed?

2. Do you have the shelf/storage space to accommodate packaging?

3. Does the cultivator have multiple packaging options?

4. What are the minimum purchasing requirements, if any?

5. How far is their facility from your shop? Would bad weather prevent them from being able to make a delivery? Would a delayed delivery be detrimental to your business?

6. Do they use a third-party delivery service?

7. Did they participate in medical markets before recreational? If not, how long have they been in business?

8. What is their delivery schedule? Will they deliver on weekends?

9. Is delivery based on first come, first served or do they have priority clients?

10. What forms of payment do they accept? What is their preferred method of payment?

11. Does the cultivator have a buyers circle?

12. What are your company values? Do they align with the cultivator's values?

13. Does the cultivator provide flower to your direct competitors? If so, how many of them?

14. What brands are trending in your shop's neighborhood?

15. Is your cultivator selling you flower at the same rate as your competitor?

16. Are they willing to provide vendor samples for shop consideration?

17. Are they willing to provide education samples for budtenders?

18. Do they use pesticides? If so, what kind? Is this a concern to your target market?

19. Have they ever had to recall their flower? If so, for what reason? How many times have they recalled product?

20. How is the flower grown (indoor, outdoor, greenhouse)? What is the harvest process? How long is the flower cured? Where is it grown?

21. Typically when are the harvest and expiration dates on their products?

▶ **Does Your Grower Pass the Test?,** continued

22. What categories of products does the company carry? Are they planning on expanding?

23. Is there a way for customers to contact the company? Does the cultivator offer vendor days?

24. Where does the vendor send products for testing? Do they use different testing facilities depending on the product category? Why did they choose that particular testing company?

25. Does the cultivator charge more for strains that test higher in THC?

26. Do they offer farm tours for shop employees?

27. Do they offer VR farm tours during vendor days for customers/patients?

28. Do they have a solid brand and brand story?

Source: Wick & Mortar.

Municipalities require all kinds of business audits from fire code audits to security audits. So before launching your brand or store to the public, you need to undergo one last round of compliance review—usually conducted by some government agency.

Before that takes place, consider hiring a third-party auditor to conduct some audits of your own—and continue to do so periodically over your first few months of activity. "These will cover all the things that can get you in trouble—all the ways to dot your Is and cross your Ts," Stratford says. "This will allow you not only to run a more efficient business but also to fix all the mistakes and avoid all the pitfalls you can before you open your doors."

It's not just about opening your doors,but about opening them the right way, he concludes. "So, to recap, go over your compliance points checklist, know that everybody knows you are going live, and be ready to flip the switch."

One of the largest compliance pitfalls derives from vendors and providers. Take a look at the sidebar above, which shares 28 questions to ask your providers. Making sure they fulfill these requirements will reduce your noncompliance risk substantially.

Before opening the doors of your store, office, grow operation, manufacturing facility, testing lab, or whatever it is you are starting, you will need to complete five main tasks:

1. Finish building and training your team.
2. Brand your company and craft a compelling story around it.

3. Get your physical location ready for business, complete with security systems and interior design.

4. Run a soft launch with friends and colleagues to assess how people interact with your space and catch any problems before opening your doors.

5. Conduct final audits, both internally and with third parties.

Now that you've gone through all the stages involved in setting up your shop, from naming and branding to the final audits, it's time to unlock your doors and let the world know you're open for business. In Chapter 8, we'll look at all things related to marketing, advertising, public relations, and media coverage.

Getting the
Word Out

Cannabis is getting more mainstream by the minute. However, getting the word out about a brand can still be quite tricky since many of the traditional marketing and advertising channels are not yet fully available to the industry.

For example, did you know you will most likely not be able to advertise a cannabis business on Facebook? Even if you never touch the plant, Mark Zuckerberg will usually not take your money—although there are some workarounds. There are online outlets that seem a little more receptive, like Twitter, LinkedIn, and YouTube, but the barriers remain high.

Since restrictions and regulations for cannabis advertising vary from one jurisdiction to another, the first thing you should do is familiarize yourself with the local laws regarding how you can market and promote your business.

Marketing and Public Relations

Once your product is in place and you know what your brand stands for and looks like, you will need to set up a proper marketing and public relations strategy. "It doesn't matter if you have the best product in the world; if the people don't know about it, your company will fail," Cynthia Salarizadeh, CEO of cannabis public relations firm Salar Media Group, says.

But how do you get the word out about your business when advertising options are so limited?

For the time being, exposure pretty much boils down to press coverage, strong alternative marketing campaigns, and robust community building through social media and physical presence.

For Celeste Miranda, founder and CEO of The Cannabis Marketing Lab, a firm serving more than 50 clients in six different countries, the most effective marketing tool in the cannabis industry is word of mouth. The agency has also had considerable success with email marketing and search engine optimization strategies. Craft a strong SEO strategy and buy good opt-in mailing lists, she recommends.

One more thing you can do to drive interest in your brand is build your own credibility and authoritative position as an influencer or media resource. Because the cannabis industry is so new, who is behind a product is, on occasion, more important than the product itself, Miranda argues.

> **tip** ⓘ
>
> Offer yourself as an interview subject to media outlets to build your influencer credibility. Make yourself available by registering at Cision's HARO (www.helpareporter.com) and AxisWire's STAR (www.axiswire.com) and respond to as many queries as possible.

So despite the limitations, "you need to be confident that you can grow your business and your clientele around those rules and regulations," Civilized's Riedle adds.

Understanding How Public Relations Work

People often see public relations and marketing as a luxury—or even a rip-of: something reserved for big companies with a lot of extra money to spend. Usually, this misconception stems from not understanding what public relations and marketing firms do, and what differentiates this work from a paid ad.

So let's discuss the difference between marketing (which includes advertising) and public relations.

Advertising is most often paid for, and you as the business owner retain control and final say over the wording, messaging, graphics, and placement. The call to action (CTA) is quite obviously to purchase the product being advertised. Public relations, on the other hand, are a bit more grassroots in nature as you are asking the media to provide coverage of your product free of charge. You do not have complete creative control with PR, but the trade-off is that your product message is being amplified by an objective party. Marketing, public relations, and getting the word out about your product constitute the second half of the business-building process, and they are arguably as important as creating a good product, building a strong team, etc. So make sure your marketing and public relations strategy aligns with your original business plan.

"There are more than 170,000 words in the English language, and the right words can make all the difference," Proven Media's vice president Neko Catanzaro says. "PR professionals can help cannabusinesses define their message and amplify it across multiple media platforms. Right now, it's easy to get 'confined' to digital tactics, but the power of print is not dead. Creating a media mix is key to a robust and dynamic PR strategy."

Public relations and marketing don't just mean connecting with the media and writing press releases. A strong PR strategy maps out all your communications for the next six to 12 months.

"Of course everything evolves and changes, but you need to plan exactly how you are going to approach unveiling your brand, unveiling new products, unveiling new features in an app, or whatever the case may be," Salarizadeh argues. "Things have to happen in a certain order. Otherwise, you'll ruin your momentum."

Entrepreneurs often don't even know what a press release is, how to write one, and why each wire service costs as much as it does. A public relations firm will take care of this for you—it's a very specific, structured exercise. However, you need to be prepared to spend a few thousand bucks a month for this service—typically between $1,500 and $10,000 per month, depending on the firm and the services you need. The highest fees will not necessarily translate into the best results; it's all about what suits your needs best.

Ultimately, what you are paying for is not the writing service or pitching an interesting angle on your story to the media. What you pay for is expertise and connections. Learning which media outlets and journalists cover which topics, and how to reach and pitch them effectively, takes a lot of time—time that would be better spent managing your business. You will have enough on your plate as it is.

"A lot of times, editors are just assigning cannabis stories to entry-level writers and one-off reporters. So it's hard to find reporters covering the industry consistently," cannabis writer Debra Borchardt says.

To overcome these challenges, "make sure to find a public relations and marketing firm that has experience in navigating the terrain of a federally illegal commodity market like cannabis is," Salarizadeh recommends. "This is like no other industry because you basically cannot pay for exposure. So a good PR agent needs to understand who to call at different publications [both cannabis-focused and mainstream] to reach certain audiences and what services can help you circumvent all of these limitations."

In other words, what you need to do is find the right public relations and marketing group for you. And make sure it's included in your budget!

"If you're not spending money on marketing, understand that your competitors probably are and you'll get crushed," The Cannabis Story Lab's John Sidline adds. He says you should plan to spend between 7 percent and 10 percent of your gross receipts on marketing and PR. With the increasing competition in the industry, marketing will not only be about getting new customers but about retaining your existing ones.

Does the Glove Fit?

A good mantra to remember is this: not all PR firms are created equal.

One firm may be great at promoting public companies, understanding the nuances of working with a business that trades on a major stock exchange; another may be impressively good at working with scarce resources, managing crises, and promoting personal and cultural brands; and a third may be best suited for startups with a couple of million dollars in the bank. You get it: it's a "different strokes for different folks" situation.

Also consider whom you'll be marketing to. Government relations-focused PR is different from consumer-focused PR or investor-focused PR. "Some publicists can manage any type of product or brand, but these are rare. Most PR agents (and I'm included here) have certain specialties. So look at their portfolio of clients, at their past work, in order to find out who's a good fit for you," Salarizadeh says. "It's all about experience—not just PR experience, but cannabis PR experience."

Public relations firms and agents who have been servicing the cannabis industry for some time (experience in the industry is *fundamental*) include:

- ▶ Bridge Strategic Communications: www.bridgestrategic.com
- ▶ The Cannabis Story Lab: http://thecannabisstorylab.com
- ▶ Cannabrand: http://cannabrand.co
- ▶ 5W Public Relations: www.5wpr.com
- ▶ GVM Communications: www.gvmcommsinc.com
- ▶ Higher Ground: www.highergroundagency.com
- ▶ KCSA Cannabis: www.kcsa-cannabis.com
- ▶ Kip Morrison & Associates: www.kipmorrison.com
- ▶ McGrath/Power: www.mcgrathpower.com
- ▶ NisonCo: http://nisonco.com
- ▶ North 6th Agency: www.n6a.com
- ▶ Potnt Agency: www.potnt.com
- ▶ Powerplant Global Strategies: http://powerplantstrategies.com
- ▶ Precise Cannabis: www.precisecannabis.com
- ▶ Proven Media: http://provenmediaservices.com
- ▶ The Rosen Group: http://rosengrouppr.com
- ▶ Rosie Mattio PR: www.rosiemattiopr.com
- ▶ Salar Media Group: www.salarmediagroup.com
- ▶ Verdant Communications: www.verdantcomm.com
- ▶ Zoe Wilder: https://zoewilder.com

The Importance of the Message

There is one thing that almost everyone in the cannabis industry agrees on: to change the public's perception of cannabis and people in the industry, education is key.

"How you present yourself to the public is very important," former New York Jets defensive end Marvin Washington explains. "Whatever you claim needs to be backed by facts or science because most of the American people don't know much about the cannabis plant.

"When I first got into the industry, my older family members and friends thought I had become a drug dealer," he adds. "You have to educate people on the medicinal benefits of the cannabis plant and the range of delivery mechanisms in order to overcome the stigma."

Along a similar line, cannabis reporter Debra Borchardt recommends you stay away from inaccurate embellishments of what your company does or has accomplished. "Only claim that your company is the only one able to do ABC, or the first company to do ABC,

▶ A Cannabis PR Case Study

So you can see what a public relations strategy should look like, Salar Media Group has shared parts of a strategy it recently implemented for Yvonne DeLaRosa Green's 99 High Tide Collective, a new dispensary in Malibu.

Strategies and Tactics

Target cannabis, finance, entrepreneurship, and business publications for features on the activity and updates on the launches concerning all areas. Targeted online and print publications, radio, and television to include, but are not limited to:

▶ *Print*: *Wired, Denver Post, Bloomberg Businessweek, Wall Street Journal, Westword, International Business Times, The Cannabist, The Gazette, Denver Business Journal, Canyon Courier, Independent, The New York Times, Los Angeles Times, LA Weekly, Chicago Tribune, USA Today, TIME, Entrepreneur, Forbes, The Economist, Wired, Fortune, High Times, Cannabis Now, Cannabis Business Times, Marijuana Venture, MG Magazine, Dope Magazine, Sensi Magazine, Freedom Leaf, Investment Now, Barron's,* etc.

▶ *Online*: Bloomberg.com, Wired, TechCrunch, Marijuana Business Daily, MJINews, Cannabis Now, MG, Forbes Online, Inc.com, The Business Journals Online, Denver Post Online, The New York Times Online, LA Weekly Online, Marijuana.com, Cannabis Industry Journal, Green Flower Media, Ladybud, Cheddar, TheStreet.com, Business Insider, BuzzFeed, Yahoo! Finance, New Cannabis Ventures, Marijuana Moment, Vice

▶ *Radio*: Cannabis Radio, Cannabis Network Radio, 420Radio, California radio stations (i.e., Los Angeles stations 104.3 MYFM-KBIG, K-LOVE 107.5 KLVE, KOST 103.5, KFI AM 640, and 95.5 KLOS, as well as San Francisco and San Diego stations) and national stations (i.e., NPR).

▶ *Television*: (CA) LA: KTLA 5, KABC 7, KTTV Fox 11; SD: KGTV 10, KFMB 8, KSWB Fox 5; SF: KRON 4, KPIX 5, KGO 7.

Internet

▶ Coordinate all messaging with digital marketing/social media plan.

▶ Coordinate all social media campaigns with the scheduled press releases.

Conferences (to be featured at or at least one of us to be present at)

▶ Marijuana Business Daily Conference November NV—LV

► A Cannabis PR Case Study, continued

Initial Timeline

Throughout the week, the PR teams will continually evolve the campaign to what works best, create and update press kit materials, distribute press releases, pitch media, provide weekly PR/marketing team calls to review activity and changes that we may want to pursue, coordinate event schedules and tie-ins, and arrange speaking engagements for all appropriate team members.

Below is a list with pitching specifics for the first month of work, which coordinate with the themes that will set the stage for the rest of the year and the brand overall.

- ► Finalize contract and payment with SMG
- ► Research editorial opportunities for the entire duration of the launch campaign on Cision
- ► Coordinate calls with writers/reporters for interviews in advance of the press release distribution
- ► Create the press kit
- ► Finalize updates on C-level biographies
- ► Build the media contact lists for the overall brand and each press release specifically (cannabis, tech, finance, business, media, entrepreneur, startups, women, etc.)
- ► Begin to contact key media for strategic story placements
- ► Finalize talking points and media prep questions

Source: Salar Media Group.

if it's true. I've had many PR people pitch me stories saying X was the *only* company to ever do something, or the *first* company to ever do something, and I would have to answer them back saying this was not really the case," she says.

"What is happening in the cannabis world right now, I think, is that nobody knows who to trust," Green Flower Media's Max Simon adds. "The truth is you develop trust by educating people on the cannabis plant or your product. People are not putting enough emphasis on producing content in their particular domain."

A final piece of advice on crafting your message comes from New Frontier Data's executive vice president of communications and government affairs, Gretchen Gailey: "It's extremely important for businesses to remember who their audience is when they are approaching the media or their customers. How you market to one consumer group is very different than how you might to another, and the same goes for different media outlets."

Imagine you wanted to sell a topical to a geriatric demographic. The way you push your message will be very different than if you were selling a sports-focused cannabis product. "The same holds true for when you are approaching the cannabis media or a more mainstream outlet like *The Washington Post*," Gailey says.

How to Reach the Media

If you plan to manage your initial public relations yourself, we recommend you start with more than 150 relatively well-known cannabis-focused publications for media coverage. Sites like HERB, *High Times*, Leafly, Civilized, The Cannabist, or Green Market Report are more likely to pick up your story at first and approach it from the right angle.

However, the rapid pace at which new cannabis products, brands, and services are emerging is making the competition for their attention fierce. So understand your niche, and find publications paying particular attention to it.

Also consider advertising on these media outlets, The Cannabis Marketing Lab's Celeste Miranda suggests. "I would look at putting both digital and print advertising there, and I would try to negotiate the price—most magazines will go down on their pricing," she discloses.

Finally, don't forget your cannabis-focused local media, podcast host Mehka King adds. "These publications are doing the work on the ground, letting people know what's going on from state to state, from city to city, (and) from person to person," he says. "And this will continue to happen as the industry grows."

Now, if reaching cannabis-focused media outlets and getting them interested in your story or product is hard, connecting with mainstream media outlets is a real bear. "The era of just mentioning the word 'cannabis' to attract media coverage is over. While we see this as a dynamic industry that is changing every day, mainstream media has done the story on cannabis legalization and now needs a new angle to be interested," New Frontier Data's Gailey contends.

Unfortunately, even when you do manage to catch their attention, there's a "giggle factor" that often hinders education while favoring extremely tired puns about cannabis businesses "budding" or "growing like weeds." So here are some things you should take into account when trying to get the right kind of coverage:

1. Understand which media outlet you should pitch each story to.
2. Identify which reporters cover topics somehow related to your brand, and figure out the best angle to pitch them.

3. Frame your stories in larger ones, or at least craft a compelling story for your brand.

4. Establish personal relationships with writers, reporters, and editors.

5. Know your public.

6. Accept your limitations; not every cannabis product is built for the mainstream or can be approached in a mainstream fashion.

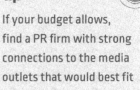

tip

If your budget allows, find a PR firm with strong connections to the media outlets that would best fit your product.

"I think we're starting to see more lifestyle reporters covering cannabis," Karen Blondell, co-founder at The Cannabis Story Lab, says. "We are seeing national and regional publications distributing lifestyle-oriented cannabis content. For instance, I recently found out about *Elevate Nevada*: it's more of a lifestyle magazine, but it's all about cannabis. What's interesting is that they are putting it out for free not in dispensaries but in places like Jamba Juice or pharmacies—places where everyday consumers are going."

One financial media outlet with extensive, serious coverage of the cannabis industry, surprisingly strong search engine positioning, and a wide distribution network that includes Yahoo!, MarketWatch, CNNMoney, Morningstar, and even Fox Business, is Benzinga. Managing editor Jason Shubnell says, "Covering marijuana has been very hot and very cold. The sector was all the rage in 2014 amid Colorado's legalization, but from a business perspective, readers soon lost interest. Reader interest peaked again in 2016 amid the presidential election."

While Shubnell still seems hesitant to cover marijuana stocks, especially those penny stocks that trade over the counter—because "any little news item can move them, while some operate under unknown or shady circumstances"—he does believe that "the medicinal push and growing acceptance have allowed more people to come forward and even create entirely new businesses from their experience with marijuana."

"It's very rewarding being able to help tell these stories," he concludes.

Fancy a Mainstream Feature?

Debra Borchardt is arguably the best-known cannabis reporter in the U.S. Until she launched her own website focused solely on cannabis industry financial news—the Green Market Report (www.greenmarketreport.com)—she wrote for more mainstream publications, publishing more than 250 articles in less than three years.

"I used to write about cannabis for publications like TheStreet.com. While the audience of these outlets is much bigger than that of cannabis-specific sites, it is also much broader in the sense that it is often not interested in the details of these stories," she says. As such, her general stories tended to do better than the deeper dives into the cannabis industry she wrote.

When editors of mainstream media outlets see these results, they tend to only want to run more general-interest stories, stories that will appeal to the broader public, Borchardt explains. This makes it particularly challenging for cannabis brands to pitch stories to them successfully.

So here's the first tip for reaching mainstream media outlets: find the right reporter and pitch broad stories about industry trends, embedding your own story in this larger trend. For example, if you are manufacturing vaporizers, don't send an email talking about the benefits of your product; instead, share some statistics about the surge in popularity of cannabis concentrates, and then show how your brand is benefiting from this trend.

"I am less interested in a one-company or single-entrepreneur stand-alone pitch. I'm more interested if the company can put its story in the context of a trend that hasn't been extensively covered already and can mention other companies that are part of this trend," Julie Weed, cannabusiness contributor at *The New York Times* and other mass media outlets, says.

Similarly, if you can link your story to a relevant news event, try to get ahead of it and pitch reporters a few days before it occurs. "For example, if you know there is going to be a tax vote and your company has some relation to the story of that tax vote, you would want to send an email to reporters in advance of the event; a reporter needs at least two or three days to work on a story," Borchardt adds.

Another very important thing to consider when pitching a reporter is to only reach out with stories that fall into his or her field of expertise. "If there is a reporter who mostly writes about cannabis from the medical point of view, then only pitch medical stories. If the reporter covers financial stories instead, he or she will be annoyed when a company pitches a story that is political or medical in nature," Borchardt says. "To me, this shows that the person pitching the idea has not taken the time to do their homework."

"Target the right journalist. I get a lot of emails every day with pitches for topics I don't cover, so I just delete them," Julie Weed concurs. "And keep emails to one screen maximum. Just give me a few sparklers: some super-short examples or some super-interesting numbers and even what the headline of the article might be.

"If I'm interested in reading the pitch, I might be interested in writing that article," she adds. "I like business topics and quirky stuff like the story about a couple of retired ladies who started a marijuana business."

► Are You @HERBworthy?

In a world where cannabis products are born and die faster than a butterfly, how do you get the attention of the most engaged cannabis community in the world? What makes a product or business worthy of HERB's coverage?

HERB looks for companies that understand their customers, comprehend why people care about them, and are clearly different in some way, founder and CEO Matt Gray explains. "There are hundreds of vaporizers, hundreds of edible products—there is a lot of stuff out there. So if you hope to get coverage (and customers), you have to make sure that you have a unique value proposition that is currently not being served in the industry.

"If you are really able to tap into that and then use the power of stories to convey that message, that's the start of a winning formula," he adds. It's all about figuring out why people should care, whether your story is compelling, and how your message will travel.

So come up with a captivating story—something that's larger than your product. As we've mentioned before, it's not so much about why your cannabis oils are great but about how you are capitalizing on a trend of increasing demand for marijuana concentrates; it's not about your new line of glass pipes but about how they can bring women between 35 and 55 years old closer to weed; and it's certainly not about your CBD cream but about how sports leagues are increasingly allowing athletes to treat their ailments with CBD-based or CBD-infused products.

"People want stories that evoke some kind of emotional reaction. People should either be heartwarmed, or intrigued, or surprised, or inspired, or amused," Gray argues. "You need some emotional reaction from your story around this product because your goal is for readers to remember you and purchase your product. Ultimately, the best scenario is to create a kind of viral loop, meaning that people see your product, they learn about it in a very succinct fashion, and then they want to share it with their friends because they feel so compelled by the need and the story that you are serving.

"When pitching HERB, reach out to individual writers who cover subjects close to what you are doing, and send a very customized email and pitch. In a very distinct and tight way, let them know why you created whatever you did, what it's all about, and why the HERB community should care," Gray says. "Make sure you have all the collateral material to make that writer's job as easy as humanly possible. These people are incredibly busy and get pitched all the time, so make sure your message is customized, well-thought-through, and with a strong subject line."

► **Are You @HERBworthy?,** continued

What about branded content, though?

In Gray's view, companies should be tapping into both sides: editorial and branded content. People can tell the difference, so both channels can benefit your brand in different ways. The editorial side is mostly for compelling stories; the branded side is more focused on getting the word out about your actual product.

"If you're doing your job right, you will get picked up by a publication like HERB because your product is so amazing. However, getting further coverage and exposure through branded content is not a bad idea as the brand has a lot more control over the messaging," he concludes.

Finally, be persistent but not overbearing. While reporters are often busy and might have missed your first email, it is unlikely they would miss three of them. So if you've pitched a reporter and did not hear back from him, you can try to reach him again. But don't flood his inbox; after a couple of unanswered messages, move on to the next journalist.

"Sometimes it's helpful when people send pitches twice in case you missed the first one or just to push it to the top of your inbox because some reporters receive over a 100 emails a day," Borchardt says. "If a pitch is news-sensitive, you can pitch again within a day as a reminder. If it's not a news event, which I think is the best way to get coverage, and it's more evergreen—which means it could stand on its own in any other time—I think you should follow up within a week and then no more for that particular pitch. Too many emails can turn off a reporter."

Print and Digital: Getting on High Times

Of the hundreds of emails that Emily Cegielski received while working as *High Times'* director of digital media only a few got opened. "There is one huge difference between what I actually look at and what gets deleted: the emails I open usually contain a piece of content that is not just about *their* product. It's something that incorporates their product, incorporates other similar products, but is also a fad, something that's actually click-y, something that does not look the same as sponsored content," she explains.

Beyond helping your brand get noticed, landing an unpaid piece on the *High Times* website shows there is value in your company's narrative or your product's story. So

Cegielski suggests getting a professional writer to work on your story and your pitch before reaching out to *High Times* and other relevant media outlets; you might only get one shot at piquing their interest.

"I very rarely look at press releases," she adds, throwing some extra wood onto the you-need-to-be-creative bonfire.

Beyond click-y content, *High Times* covers very good interviews and stories, Cegielski says. "We will be especially inclined to publishing a story if the company offers the story for free and provides photos or video links. When we get an article like that, we push it out across our social media."

Getting in *High Times'* print version is a bit harder. Many times, the process starts with getting on hightimes.com.

"The magazine process is very different. To get your product on there, you should consider reaching out directly to the magazine editors and sending samples to the office," Cegielski says. "We are never going to write about a product that we haven't tested personally.

"Probably the biggest piece of advice I would have for a new pot entrepreneur looking to get media attention is: do a good networking exercise and connect with the people in the media. Any editor is more likely to respond to you if you have a personal connection with him or her even if you just met one time or talked over the phone or interacted on social media exchanging a few witty comments," she adds. "Develop a rapport with people."

Social Media

These days, it's not just traditional media that will help you get the word out about your brand. Social media is incredibly important as well. In fact, presenting a strong story and image on social media can lead to a very successful brand, while a weak social media strategy can doom it to oblivion.

Almost every cannabis brand (with a few exceptions) should have a Facebook page, an Instagram account, and a Twitter handle. "Having a website is also great, but Instagram can be more useful at times," *High Times'* Emily Cegielski says.

According to Cegielski, Twitter is the most lenient of the three social networks mentioned above in terms of the type of content it allows. However, Instagram can be more useful when trying to build a community and convert users into customers. "You will be fine posting pictures of weed on Instagram; just stay away from photos of trashy girls using skimpy clothes and things like that," she says. "I've seen a lot of Instagram accounts get closed for that."

In fact, Facebook and Instagram are notorious for shutting down cannabis-related accounts. Christine Young, owner of one of the most popular cannabis newsfeeds on Twitter, WeedFeed, and social media manager for Cresco Labs and Cresco Yeltrah, confirms this.

"At the end of the day, brands can create attention by doing something flashy, but they can only create loyalty by making customers believe in their product," High Pressure Zone's JJ Kaye says. "Building out a channel on social media that clearly tells your story is as important as building a community and cultivating a sense of interest and ownership."

It's all about posting and generating engagement, he adds, pointing out that the best communities are built organically—meaning you shouldn't worry about not being able to pay Facebook or Instagram to promote your posts.

"For someone who is looking to do social marketing/promotion organically, finding the most popular hashtags on Instagram and Twitter could be a relevant starting spot," Brent Slava, head of Benzinga's newsdesk, says. "From there, they would want to find a way to create interesting posts that could pique the interest of those social users browsing through popular hashtags."

"But it takes time to build a strong brand on social media, and the ROI might not be obvious at first," WeedFeed's Christine Young adds. "Think of it as building relationships with potential customers and also with influencers who can help you spread your message. Your content needs to be as good as possible so people will want to share it."

That said, always follow the terms of service for whatever social media platform you are using. Losing your account could end up being very costly for your brand.

The Full Ecosystem

Beyond establishing a presence on social media, consider building an ecosystem that includes real-life activation through presence on the ground and then amplifying this reach via social media.

"You can't just have a social media-only company or a digital-only company; you need to have that physical presence to create visibility and content for your social networks," Kaye says. "There is a synchronicity between engaging people in real life and re-engaging them online."

At the same time, you cannot just promote yourself 24-7. "There is a human and humanitarian aspect to the cannabis industry," Celeste Miranda warns. "To hold your audience's attention, you need to remain involved, share news, give back to the industry."

"Don't use your social media platforms just to sell your product but also to provide interesting things that make people want to come back," Cegielski concurs.

As we mentioned above, not every product is suited for social media. But for those that are, there are a few ways to get Facebook to advertise your cannabis products. You have to be creative and come up with options, alternative landing pages, etc., Miranda explains, adding that most of these methods are sort of trade secrets for which you'll have to pay.

Finally, consider contests and giveaways as well as video content. "We've had success with these strategies," she says.

"People will likely spend more time on a video than on a written piece," John Sidline agrees.

Ways to Engage Customers

After getting the word out about your brand or product, you'll need to find ways to keep customers engaged. As you might expect, several companies offer engagement services. A few such firms are:

- ▶ Baker Technologies (www.trybaker.com) uses an online platform to generate foot traffic, repeat visits, and customer loyalty.
- ▶ The Daily Leaf (http://dailyleafdeals.com) offers deals and discounts on its site to direct new customers your way.
- ▶ Green Marimba (www.greenmarimba.com) uses SMS to get new customers through your doors.
- ▶ SpringBig (https://www.springbig.com/) offers a similar SMS marketing service.

Beyond these services, cannabis brands need to be creative when engaging customers. One of the most effective ways to reach new clients and foster loyalty among existing ones is knowing and appealing to what they like.

Take the following example: a recent study conducted by Green Market Report in conjunction with Consumer Research Around Cannabis and Local Sports Insights revealed that legal cannabis consumers follow pro football (the NFL) more than any other sport. So why not create promotions around NFL game nights or find a current or former NFL player to endorse your brand? Check out the graphic in Figure 8–1 on page 151 to see more data from the study.

Especially taking into account that advertising options for cannabis businesses are limited, whatever a company decides to communicate has to be well-thought-out. Understanding how cannabis users are consuming media can help you target them. Along with that, entrepreneurs need to know the unique attributes of the local market in which they operate.

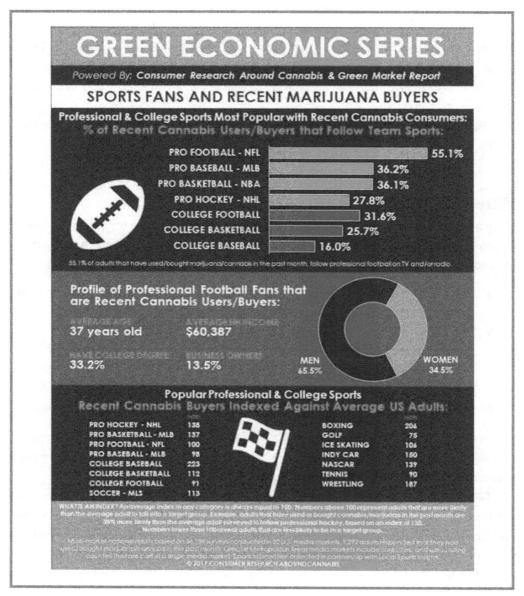

FIGURE 8–1: **Sports Fan and Recent Marijuana Buyers**

Source: Green Market Report. Find it at www.greenmarketreport.com/touchdown-cannabis-consumers-prefer-the-nfl-over-all-other-pro-sports.

"In Los Angeles, a good marketing strategy might be aligning your business in some way with a sports product, because sports are big out there. In Denver, instead, a company's marketing strategy might be more effective if it is linked to leisure activities because Colorado is a snow/ski portal. So understanding what makes each market unique is very important," Consumer Research Around Cannabis' vice president Jeffrey Stein points out.

Consumer profile data is emerging in the cannabis industry. This makes it easier for brands to figure out how to reach their customers, Green Market Report co-founder Cynthia Salarizadeh says. "So if I had a brand that was geared more toward women, I probably wouldn't go after the NFL crew. Instead, I would try and get my story on *Nylon* magazine, *Vogue*, etc. What's important is to figure out what your target consumer is, what they like, which sites they frequent online . . ."

Celebrity Endorsements

One more way to get the word out about your company is through celebrity endorsements, which are becoming increasingly popular in the cannabis space.

"Celebrities and athletes can bring a lot of attention and focus to any issues that they get involved in," former NFL player Marvin Washington says. "However, you need to be careful. Make sure that there is a depth of knowledge there and that they are not just promoting a product that they don't believe in.

"Unlike other industries, most of the celebrities getting involved in the cannabis space really believe in it and its potential to reduce the harmful effects of pharmaceuticals. This makes celebrity endorsements in this space much more legitimate than in others, like when you have athletes endorsing beer, soda, or something like that," he adds. So if you want to get a celebrity behind your product, make sure he believes in it and would use it personally, if applicable, he concludes.

"In my case, I didn't want the focus of the brand to be put on Blues Traveler. You should try to create what you want to create and make it stand on its own two feet," Brendan Hill adds, arguing that celebrity endorsements should help you build your brand but not define it. "With a lot of celebrity endorsements, if you don't hit it out of the park, you just wasted an opportunity. I think it's better if you don't use celebrity endorsements to open the door for you. It should be more of a cool extra."

"In a competitive market with no clear established brands, a celebrity endorsement can garner attention, but it can be fleeting," Canna Ventures' Eric Layland says. "Additionally, those celebrities who have come out of the green closet may have qualities that don't connect well with the intended audience."

Take Snoop Dogg as an example, he suggests. Snoop is a "charismatic and astute businessman and brand." However, his endorsement will not resonate with every audience, nor will it relate to the qualities of every brand.

However, some people, like Celeste Miranda, believe celebrity endorsements are not worth the money. "A lot of people are surprised by this, but I think that the return on investment is not worth it. With where the industry is right now, I think there are so many areas to better use your marketing dollars," she says.

Rather than celebrity endorsements, brands should consider aligning with causes, Layland suggests. "Celebrities can run their course and might not always be a positive," he says. "A cause can be leveraged to support a broader base of potential consumers with a deeper sense of loyalty to the brand because the brand supports what's important to them."

As mentioned at the beginning of this chapter, there is no use in having a great brand or product if nobody knows about it. So getting the word out about your company may be as important as having a business in the first place.

To effectively communicate your message, turn to public relations and marketing firms—especially taking into account the restrictions cannabis businesses face in terms of advertising possibilities.

In addition, get acquainted with the media landscape and target the right publications and reporters for coverage. Finally, do not underestimate the importance of social media and physical presence; these days people like to see things in real life and then re-engage with them online.

Common Post-Startup Issues

Although Gateway's Ben Larson can share innumerable pieces of advice for cannabis entrepreneurs, there is one he repeats like a broken record—and for good reason: "For God's sake, don't get in legal trouble; always stay on top of everything that's going on."

Setting up a cannabis business is complicated. However, the challenges will not end when you open your doors. In fact, remaining compliant while in operation is also very demanding. As per Marijuana Business Daily, the top challenges that at least one in three cannabis businesses face are federal laws, compliance, and scalability/growth.

Make sure you have a really solid understanding of compliance requirements and have a compliance program in place. "Consult with your legal counsel, your accountants, and any other professional you are working with. Spend the money necessary to ensure you have these compliance programs in place," GreenWave Advisors' Matt Karnes recommends. "If there is just one deviation from the regulations, it could be reason for regulators to come and shut you down for not being in compliance with the law."

One of the most useful moves you can make is to establish relationships with regulators and regulatory agencies, Green Flower Media's Max Simon and the California Bureau of Cannabis Control's Amelia Hicks both suggest. Even if bureaucracy seems impersonal, remember that all agencies are made up by people who will appreciate that you are interested in remaining compliant and try to make their job easier.

But what type of problems should you look out for?

Watch Your Back

According to Anne Van Leynseele, there are two major liabilities in any business, marijuana-related or not: employees and taxes.

One relatively easy-to-remember (and apply) rule of thumb is this: as soon as you make your first dollar, you should start saving 10 percent of your revenue for emergencies and fluctuations in cash flow, and another 40 percent for taxes. Almost everything that's left (at least during the first few years) should be allocated to funding your operations, rather than returning cash to the founders.

"We find that licensed businesses are particularly vulnerable to disgruntled employees," Van Leynseele says. "Most of the regulatory agencies right now are so overloaded with work that they are responding only to complaints, and the largest source of complaints are disgruntled employees."

One way to handle this is to avoid what is often referred to as the "living room culture" prevalent in the cannabis industry. This means you should be careful when deciding what facets of your operation you will share with your employees and what you should keep to yourself. Revealing financial information, payroll data, and other numbers to your subordinates can come back to haunt you later down the road.

Another big source of legal issues is disputes among partners. "Most of the failures that we have seen so far stem from internal issues—from partners fighting," Bradley Blommer of Green Light Law Group says. So as we said earlier, make certain your partners' views and goals align with yours before going into business with them.

Bankruptcy and Receivership

The laws and regulations that apply to cannabis businesses are often complex and can conflict on diverse levels. We cannot stress enough that you should get guidance from professionals who are constantly keeping track of every change in legislation and regulation.

One of the biggest problems for cannabis businesses is the current inability to file for bankruptcy because this sort of protection works on a federal level. However, in case of insolvency, marijuana businesses can recur to a state-level receivership, which basically implies the court will appoint someone else to run your company, avoiding liquidation, or will decide to auction your assets.

"The whole purpose of bankruptcy or receivership is to cleanse all of the prior sins of a company and start with a fresh slate," Anne Van Leynseele explains. So receivership is a necessary resource for states where there is a limited number of licenses for cannabis businesses. "Nobody will want to touch a tainted license, so mechanisms to cleanse them are necessary," she adds.

Navigating Turbulent Waters

Cannabis waters can be turbulent, so always remain on the safe side. Beyond the issues mentioned above, "remaining compliant is not rocket science," Green Light Law Group's Bradley Blommer says—almost joking. "Just don't sell weed to kids, only trade with licensed and authorized businesses . . . those kinds of basic things."

Any order you get, any client that comes through the door, check their credentials; you could lose your whole business just to avoid losing a few thousand dollars.

"Whether it's a vendor, a client, a partner, a supplier, or an advisor, you need to check they are compliant as well because they impact your own business and compliance," MJIC's CEO Sturges Karban agrees. "Also in this line, another trip wire hiding in plain sight is advertising. Even if you sell ancillaries, be careful."

Here are a few compliance questions for you to think about:

- ▶ Are your customers old enough to buy from you?
- ▶ Do they have an ID to prove it?
- ▶ Do they have a medical marijuana card, if needed?
- ▶ Are your vendors and providers licensed?

- ▶ Do they have the paperwork to prove it?
- ▶ Are all their products properly tested?
- ▶ Is their packaging compliant?
- ▶ Are they fulfilling labeling and childproofing requirements?
- ▶ Are the delivery/distribution services your vendors use licensed as well?

One more great challenge is posed by stigma. "People don't see cannabis or the people behind cannabis with any lens of accuracy. And that includes the lawmakers, the policy-makers, the local councils, and all the people that are attempting to regulate this market and this space," Green Flower Media's Max Simon says.

"So for companies that have to deal with any form of government, whether it's regulators, local municipalities, banks, or insurance people, it's important to build relationships and get to know people from an authentic space. Show them who you are and what you are all about."

Planning Ahead

Most experts in the U.S. cannabis industry believe that, sooner or later, cannabis will be federally legal. It's a matter of when rather than if.

You'd assume that cannabis becoming federally legal would make compliance easier. But this will not be the case in every sphere. Federal legality will bring new requirements: workers' comp, OSHA guidelines, Environmental Protection Agency (EPA) obligations, consumer protection standards, etc.

And even if cannabis doesn't become federally legal any time soon, the case for ever-evolving regulation is still valid. "Rules will continue to change quite often as regulators get a better sense of how to regulate the industry," Sturges Karban says. "We are the canaries in the coal mine. So do not assume that because you are in compliance with one set of regulations today, you will be tomorrow because those regulations may no longer be in place."

> **tip**
>
> Remember: Remaining ⓘ compliant is not just about your business; it's a responsibility you have to the entire cannabis industry. Wrongdoing from a few bad actors can taint everyone in the industry.

Experts recommend that you try to anticipate which regulations will come into effect and get familiar with their requirements beforehand. "This shows a level of maturity and forward planning that is unique," Viridian Capital Advisors' Scott Greiper says.

You should also plan for the expansion of recreational markets. "When the recreational market comes into a state, it disrupts the growth of medical marijuana businesses," GreenWave Advisors' Matt Karnes says. "What we are seeing is that these markets are combining into one market in those states because it is not practical to have both."

So if you go for a medical license, take into account that your business will be grandfathered into the recreational system when its day arrives in your state, and plan accordingly.

Paying Taxes

As a legal business, you have to pay taxes. There is no way around this even though some unscrupulous consultants will tell you there is. Even if you believed that, legally, you didn't have to pay taxes, think of it as a moral obligation. You've reaped the benefits of this society and its social contract to the point where you were able to start a business of your own, so why not help the state continue to provide these opportunities to other people who deserve them as much as you do?

Now, if you think filing your personal taxes is difficult, confusing, and boring, doing the same for a cannabis business takes it to a whole new level. So hire a CPA or tax accountant to do it for you.

"Less than 1 percent of small businesses in the United States are audited by the IRS. Contrast that with the fact that 16 percent of cannabis businesses are being audited by the IRS," Anne Van Leynseele points out.

So definitely pay your taxes in full. "Make sure to pay all of your personal income taxes, payroll taxes, property taxes, etc.," cannabis activist Jodie Emery says.

Remaining compliant will pose some very specific challenges. "Sometimes it can be hard to pay your taxes with cash, but make sure to do it anyways. We all know that Al Capone got caught for tax evasion, so paying taxes is something you should do consistently," Emery continues. "The government will take your money whether you made it legally or illegally. So always pay your taxes."

Below are a few links related to cannabis taxes you might find useful:

- ▶ "Tax Guide for Cannabis Businesses" from the California Department of Tax and Fee Administration: www.cdtfa.ca.gov/industry/cannabis.htm
- ▶ IRS Tax Code 280E: www.law.cornell.edu/uscode/text/26/280E
- ▶ A directory of accounting firms servicing marijuana businesses: www.ganjapreneur.com/marijuana-accounting-firms
- ▶ Another directory of accounting firms: https://industrydirectory.mjbizdaily.com/accounting

▶ "FAQs on Taxes" from the Washington State Liquor and Cannabis Board: https://lcb.wa.gov/mj2015/faqs-on-taxes

▶ An overview of recreational marijuana taxes from the Oregon Department of Revenue: www.oregon.gov/dor/press/documents/marijuana_fact_sheet.pdf

▶ "FAQs for Marijuana Establishments" from the State of Nevada Department of Taxation: https://tax.nv.gov/FAQs/Retail_Marijuana

▶ An article explaining how to mitigate 280E tax burdens: www.ganjapreneur.com/cannabis-taxes-strategies-mitigating-section-280e

▶ Alaska's Department of Revenue's marijuana tax site: http://tax.alaska.gov/programs/programs/index.aspx?60000

Compliance: The Never-Ending Concern

Finally, as you prepare for possible pitfalls during the first few years of business, keep in mind that the biggest one may very well be compliance. Because compliance requirements can modify based on law (which can change quickly), you'll want to stay abreast of all compliance issues that could unwittingly sink your business. There is nothing fun about compliance, but there are few things more important in the cannabis industry. So to stay on the safe side, check every box in the list below:

▶ Pay attention to federal, state, and local regulations.

▶ Pay all your taxes. All of them!

▶ Be good to your employees.

▶ Pick your partners wisely.

▶ Have clear legal documentation for everything you do.

▶ Vet every customer, vendor, and partner.

▶ Have a contingency plan in case things go south.

▶ Try to anticipate which new regulations will kick in soon.

All in all, just remain compliant. Always. Never drop the ball, especially when it comes to dealing with licensed businesses or minors. Beyond that, get expert advice; it's the best way to avoid pitfalls. All this might sound boring, but it marks the difference between being shut down and running a successful cannabis business.

In our next chapter, we'll look at the main things you should take into account when growing your business and expanding to multiple locations, states, or even countries.

CHAPTER

10

Growing and Becoming a Multilocation or Multistate Company

Let's suppose that by now you have a business going, some happy customers, and a little media coverage—while always remaining compliant. What's next?

"There is a big difference from going from a small company to the rapid growth phase," says Michael Gorenstein,

CEO of the Cronos Group, one of the largest marijuana companies in the world with a market capitalization of more than $700 million as of 2017.

"In a small startup, everyone in the company kind of does everything—everyone kind of fills in where it's needed," he says. "But as you scale, it's really important to put in a framework and a structure that allows you to push down accountability, think about how you are going to deal with internal communications, and how you can make sure that the huge range of tasks and issues that come up can be dealt with in a very effective and clear manner."

You'll need to start to clearly define roles and responsibilities and start to allocate territories. Expanding to multiple states might not represent a big challenge for ancillary businesses, but plant-touching businesses will have a really hard time.

"Manage growth smartly as many bite off more than they can chew," Alan Brochstein, founder of New Cannabis Ventures, says. Even big brands face this problem. "For instance, [California cannabis dispensary] Harborside expanded into Oregon but then retrenched. Similarly, [Colorado infused products company] Dixie Brands went into Arizona and pulled out.

"Another piece of advice that is near and dear to my heart is to be very cautious of doing deals with companies on the OTC," he adds. "There is no quicker way to ruin one's reputation than by announcing an alliance with a company that turns out to be a pump and dump."

"In my opinion, growing your business and doing so appropriately in the cannabis industry is possibly even more important than your idea or concept," Dr. Bryan Doner, CEO and co-founder of Compassionate Certification Centers, says. "Building your brand and reputation within the industry and the public is imperative, and I don't think this ever stops.

"As a cannabis industry investor and business founder, things can get away from you pretty quickly if you are not careful. All of the hard work, time, and money you have invested can result in an overwhelming amount of interest in your company/product/ offering, which in itself is fantastic but oftentimes in reality can become overwhelming. Be ready for the brand you are building to go big time as those critical opportunities are few and far between," he concludes.

Differentiate

The cannabis industry is a very social one. "It's very much of a headline-oriented industry," Viridian Capital Advisors' Scott Greiper explains. "Because this is a social industry at its core, people care about what other people think about your product."

This means that as you get ready to grow, having positive testimonials from customers and business partners can do a lot for you. Get these quotes on your website and your marketing material. In addition, try to get some coverage from industry-specific media outlets like *Marijuana Business Daily*, *High Times*, *CannaInvestor* magazine, Leafly, HERB, or Green Market Report.

"As usual, every company sells features and benefits no matter if you're Tesla or Apple," Greiper adds. So very clearly communicate what's special about your product or service and what features really differentiate it from the rest. Is it cheaper? Is it manufactured in an ISO-approved facility? Is it organic? Is it more efficacious?

Ways to differentiate your business include:

▶ A unique product
▶ Organic certifications
▶ Great packaging
▶ Competitive pricing
▶ High quality
▶ 24/7 customer service
▶ Regional offices
▶ Dedicated account managers
▶ ISO approval
▶ Online tracking
▶ Subscription to blockchain control services
▶ Cryptocurrency integration

"I find that not enough companies do a good enough competitive landscape of what they are offering, who are their competitors, what is the feat of benefits from their product, and how they really differentiate," Greiper says. "Both consumers and investors need to understand the competitive landscape and where you really differentiate."

But keep in mind the differentiation gap can close quickly. So think ahead; plan how you will maintain the gap over time and avoid larger competitors incorporating your ideas into their products, ultimately wiping you off the map.

"It's always great to market off success," Greiper says. "So if early stage companies have raised money from family and friends, tested their product, and got people to raise their hands in testimony of their value—there are a lot of public relations and investor relations ways to leverage that; that then speaks to investors for a potential Series A raise."

Investors have a crowd mentality, just like consumers. "So if investors suddenly see a lot of people in the industry raising their hands and speaking on behalf of your product, then it's the old 'Peter Lynch and Fidelity Model,'" Greiper says.

If you're wondering what this model looks like, imagine you're an individual investor, not a professional money manager, and you want to know what to invest in. What Peter Lynch suggested back in the 1980s was to go to the supermarket and see what brands were flying off the shelves. "That product is being bought instead of the one on the shelf right next to it for a reason," Greiper concludes.

Raise More Money

From all this, one further piece of advice to scale your business derives: raise additional money. For more detailed information on how to conduct raises and where to find people or firms willing to invest in cannabis businesses, see Chapters 4 and 5.

"Scaling and tackling additional markets traditionally requires significant capital, which has only in the last few years become more available not only from family office investment groups but more recently traditional venture capital firms," Headset's Cy Scott says. "Having fundraising options, combined with the immediate opportunity of new markets in regions like California and Canada, makes this the opportune time to start or grow your company in this fast-moving industry."

"You probably won't be able to pinpoint the exact time your business takes hold and starts to go to the next level. But when it comes, there is no stopping it," Compassionate Certification Centers' Dr. Bryan Doner adds. "The single biggest limiting factor when that time comes will be money and how much cash on hand do you have. Your expansion/ growth and time to do so will be directly correlated to how much money you have access to then and there, at that moment."

"When you are raising money to grow and ramp up capacity, you should think of who the capital comes from," Gorenstein cautions. "If you get helpful, well-connected investors in early, they will work to help you grow your company—and you won't even need to pay them."

"When it comes to raising capital, if it sounds too good to be true, then it likely is," 420 Investor's Alan Brochstein contends. "Also, be very careful. Sometimes it's better to raise capital from a smart partner who will contribute in other ways, but maybe on somewhat less favorable terms, than one who will constantly pressure the company to show quick, short-term gains."

Get More Help

Beyond clearly differentiating your company's features and benefits, leveraging your early users, and getting that information out to the media, find help! And we don't mean just your original team but rather additional, specialized help from people with experience scaling up businesses and managing complex operations.

We can't stress this enough, and neither could the industry experts we interviewed. It's rare among early stage entrepreneurs, especially those with little experience in the field, to admit they need help. CanopyBoulder's Micah Tapman likes to tell a story: whenever he gives a talk and asks entrepreneurs how many of them think their company has problems or needs help, about 10 or 20 percent of them raise their hands. But he argues it should be all of them.

Recognizing your need for assistance early on will likely provide you an edge over your peers. As your business grows, you will need guidance not only with basic tasks but also with more complex things like advanced ordering, volume pricing discounts, and daily operations. These may seem simple tasks at first sight, but anyone running a large business can tell you complexity surges exponentially with scale.

To understand how to solve a problem, like the ones that arise with scaling up a business, entrepreneurs need to start by asking themselves the right questions. Segment these questions into smaller ones, and "you will immediately see the solution to that particular problem and figure out who can help you in solving this problem," CannaSOS' Daniel Cheine says.

So make sure that as you grow your business, you add the right people to your team. "In my opinion, this cannot be emphasized enough," Compassionate Certification Centers' Dr. Bryan Doner adds. "Always remember that you can't do it all yourself and that the most successful startup organizations have a clear goal in mind from which they do not deviate, and they divide and conquer among the ranks. Being able to delegate to the appropriate person is key to keeping up as your business grows. Be fluid in a fluid industry. Things can change quickly in cannabis, and be ready to adjust accordingly and on the fly."

At this point, you might find that you need a chief operating officer (or COO)—not to represent the company day to day (that's the CEO's job)—but to be in charge of daily operational issues.

"That is where early stage companies get into trouble," Viridian Capital Advisors' Scott Greiper says. "Entrepreneurs are thick-headed by nature. They want to maintain control, and they think they know how to do it better than anybody else. If it wasn't the case, most early stage companies would die because it's not easy to run a business. You have to have that hardheaded ego. Getting help almost goes against the grain of the moxie required to be a successful entrepreneur, but you need to deal with it."

In the end, the entrepreneur who realizes he can't do it all on his own is the most likely to succeed. Building a board of directors or advisors that will sit down once every three months to discuss the basics of your business does not really count as day-to-day, operational help.

"A COO to me is crucial to manage internal planning," the Cronos Group's Michael Gorenstein agrees. "But you will also need to start laying out other departments [at this stage]. If you focus too much on one area and leave a gap, any single area that you leave can cripple your business. If you don't have your marketing department beefed up and ready to go (even if you are using an agency), when you launch your product in additional territories, implementing the details (logos, fonts, themes, messages) will be hard. You need a marketing department to do that."

The same logic applies to other departments like hiring a CFO to oversee the finance branch and putting a good sales force together. As more capital starts flowing into your company, the amount and variety of taxes, the complexity of your payroll, the benefits your employees receive, etc. will all become harder to track. "I think the way to do this is to start to balance; you want to build out each department kind of in parallel," Gorenstein says.

Be advised that you will need to lay out some money and offer equity incentives to bring in the right kind of management talent.

"It's the operating issues that bite companies in the ass as they grow," Greiper adds. "One of the largest challenges of growth is dealing with operations, execution, ordering, manufacturing, supply chain, purchasing. That tends to suffocate early stage companies."

Furthermore, many investors have pointed out that seeing entrepreneurs get help and build a team shows maturity, which is usually what persuades them to risk capital on a venture.

Fundamentally, Gorenstein recommends putting a strong midlevel management team together. "You can't overburden yourself or your team. There is a certain limit to how many people you want to report to you," he says.

Customer Service

One of the key components driving the growth of cannabis companies, whether they are selling software or vaporizers, is good customer service. So from the very moment you get your first customer, start allocating resources to customer service.

"Customer service is so important in this industry because, as I mentioned earlier, word of mouth is so important," Celeste Miranda explains. So if people are happy with the service you offer, they are likely to recommend it to their friends, family, and even co-workers.

"Customer service should be your number-one focus," The Green Solution's co-founder and CEO, Kyle Speidell, agrees. "This is not a business where you are trying to get the most out of a customer like you would as a car salesman. A customer [of a retail company like The Green Solution] doesn't come only once a year; the majority of patrons come once a week, if not more, and it is important for them to have consistent and high-quality visits. You must work hard to ensure they are comfortable in their environment and with the products you are selling each and every day."

"Answering every call with a warm voice, answering every email (that isn't promotional) that comes into your inbox, and constantly trying to bring more value than what you receive will have a great impact on you personally, but more importantly, on your brand," CannaSOS' Daniel Cheine adds. "I personally spend three to six hours every day (sometimes literally the whole day) just answering emails, either from the support side or business development or any email that pops up in my inbox. . . . It might be agonizing to spend a lot of your day doing customer service, but if you don't put a lot of effort into improving your customer service—even if you don't answer any emails from businesses—no one is going to do business with you because they will see you as a person/brand who doesn't care about anyone and one that won't care in the future. No one likes those people."

Give Back

While many companies in the cannabis industry are focused on returning money to their investors, some of the most successful have made it their mission to return something to the community, to nurture the industry, or to fund legalization movements. Cannabis Culture, for example, invests much of the money it makes back into advocacy, providing legal help to people of scarce resources accused of cannabis-related crimes, funding cannabis education or rallies around the world, etc.

Here are a few ways cannabis businesses can serve their communities:

- ▶ Employ war veterans
- ▶ Employ people who use cannabis to medicate for serious medical conditions
- ▶ Donate to nonprofit organizations
- ▶ Organize pro-legalization rallies
- ▶ Support pro-legalization movements in nonlegal states
- ▶ Host educational events for the community
- ▶ Give free medical cannabis to those who cannot afford it
- ▶ Employ people who were convicted of simple possession of marijuana
- ▶ Throw fun events for sick kids
- ▶ Invest in online education programs

- ► Lobby to get cannabis taxes used to build schools and hospitals
- ► Create programs to combat opioid addiction

So when you find some success, in any capacity, "it would really benefit you and everyone if you decided to give something back or help people get justice—give them

► Meet Cura Cannabis Solutions

Cura Cannabis Solutions is one of the biggest cannabis brands in the United States. The company manufactures cannabis oils and has managed to amass a 20 percent market share in Oregon, doubling its size every month between April and December 2016—ending the year with 20 times the revenue it had in April. Over the first three quarters of 2017, monthly sales quadrupled as well.

So what determined the success of this company that, unlike most others in the industry, has chosen to remain horizontal and focused on oils instead of pursuing vertical integration or expanding its portfolio to include products beyond the concentrates category?

The number-one factor that determined Cura Cannabis Solutions' success was passion, Forni says. "Find your strengths and partner up with someone who fills your gaps. It's very rare to see venture capitalists fund a single-founder company."

Everything started with Cameron Forni researching vaporization to help a friend and business partner who suffered from Barrett's esophagus—which meant he could not smoke weed. "We bought every vaporizer we could get our hands on and studied how they worked," he remembers.

At one point, they found out that some of the components in the existing vape cartridges were carcinogenic—or at least detrimental to people's health—so they decided to research the options. "We finally came across a design that had no hazardous components. So we ordered a few hundred vape cartridges and started filling these up with oil from a producer we knew in my living room and selling them online," Forni continues.

It took $44,000 in cash and $66,000 in credit card debt to get the business going. The entrepreneurs paid off the full credit card debt in less than three months.

Perseverance took Forni's venture (called Select Stains at the time) to a point where a guy with a strong startup and management background noticed it and got interested in getting involved.

▶ Meet Cura Cannabis Solutions, continued

But how did Cura Cannabis Solutions grow from a living-room company into a multimillion-dollar business? The first thing that drove Cura's growth was an extremely clear vision and mission.

"Our mission is to be the leading provider of cannabis oil to both consumers and premium edible brands in legal U.S. and international markets. We are the largest cannabis oil company in Oregon, with operations up and running across California and newly legal Nevada," the company's website reads as soon as one lands on the homepage.

The second thing Cura Cannabis Solutions really believes in is people, the co-founders say, explaining they have a thorough hiring process and numerous employee-wellbeing policies in place.

A final element in Cura's success was cautious expansion. "We were never going to expand beyond Oregon until we absolutely felt like we were hitting at all cylinders there," a high-level exec in the company says. "People want to do vertical integration: they want to do candy in Oregon but grow in California. . . . That is a hard mission focus. If you want a retail store in Oregon, and you want a gummy company in Nevada, and you want a grow operation in California, I ask: who are you? What do you want to be when you grow up? How do you give a clear message to investors, customers, and vendors?

"While this might be a good income strategy, it is not a wealth-creation strategy; it is not a company-building strategy. That is why I'm tying all this together: your mission has to be clear, the people that you hire have to believe in that mission, and then you should only grow, especially in a regulated industry like cannabis, at a speed that's appropriate."

Once they hit a 50 percent market share for vape cartridges in Oregon, Forni and his team decided the time had come to ramp up hiring and evaluate what getting into the California market would look like. This led Forni to move out to California to establish the business.

Within seven months, Cura had become the third-largest cannabis company in California, so the partners decided to replicate the model in Nevada.

"Do what you are doing really, really well and keep your promises and your customers happy. This is the way to expand," the aforementioned exec concludes. "If you are in the cannabis industry for the right reasons, you should be in it for the long run—not just a couple of years."

For the full story behind Cura Cannabis Solutions, check out the exclusive article at http://entm. ag/46j.

opportunity when the government or the legal system have deprived them of it because of their involvement with cannabis in the past," Cannabis Culture's Jodie Emery recommends. Helping the community creates additional awareness around your brand, sympathy among the public and, simply put, an innate desire in others to help you help others.

Going Multilocation

How does one grow a cannabis business from a single store into a multilocation company? How does a nonretailer (like a software company, a wholesale business, a consultant, etc.) expand its reach?

Two of the most important elements in this stage of growth are good public relations and good media coverage. As you saw in Chapter 8, pick a PR agency that knows the industry and fits your specific needs to help you get mainstream media coverage. Destigmatization and education are crucial to getting people to understand that cannabis is not about getting high but about medicine, social justice, inclusion, tax revenue, crime prevention, etc. All this is central to reaching consumers beyond those immersed in the so-called "stoner culture" as well. And, ultimately, it is very likely that the mainstream customers will fuel your growth once you've passed your initial phase of development and reached most of the regular cannabis consumers that might be interested in your product.

According to Marijuana Business Daily, if you are already at the point of opening multiple locations, it is less likely you'll have to struggle to get financed.

Before moving on, it's important to highlight that licensed operators, infused products manufacturers, and so-called OTF (other than flower) product companies, including vape pens and edibles makers, are restricted to doing business within the state they are located in. Businesses that are not licensed and/or don't sell infused products and OTFs can do business in any state and around the world.

"Companies that provide technology solutions, compliance systems and software, quality and safety testing, ecommerce platforms, and any business service can operate anywhere without restriction as they do not touch the plant and do not transport federally illegal products over state lines," explains Phyto Partners' Larry Schnurmacher.

"We have seen many product companies that would be great national brands, but the capital and infrastructure required to expand outside the territory they are licensed in or conduct business in is prohibitive," he adds. "All aspects of the business, from sourcing to production, need to be replicated in each new state. It becomes difficult if not impossible to create economies of scale and streamlined systems logistics that are identical."

"You also have to make sure that, as you expand, you are maintaining your company culture," the Cronos Group's Michael Gorenstein adds.

Another key point here is consistency. "You will want to be like McDonald's where every cheeseburger is the same," The Cannabis Marketing Lab's Celeste Miranda says. "Many companies in the cannabis industry want to go multistate but cannot keep their products consistent even in their own states."

"Maintaining your quality is crucial. Your early adopters will be very vocal about your quality, so you need to maintain a relationship with them—think of them almost as part of the company," Gorenstein suggests. "If you start to scale and start making sacrifices on quality, it will have a ripple effect and eventually ruin all the brand awareness you had created."

At this point, or even earlier, you will "need to decrease, through efficiency, your cost of production in order to offset declining prices in the industry," Scott Greiper says. "This means you will have to get better at manufacturing or producing your product or service to counteract the pricing pressures."

Data from New Leaf Data Services' Cannabis Benchmarks shows that legal marijuana markets are commoditizing, and industry participants with exposure to wholesale price risk need to be prepared. "As markets mature, so do the mechanisms for managing price risk," New Leaf Data's CEO, Jonathan Rubin, explains. "Right now, most growers and retailers rely on internal practices, such as inventory management and large cash reserves, to manage price risk. We are beginning to see brokers replace individual buyers and sellers as counterparties. Eventually, we will likely see exchange-based markets—similar to those for soybeans, wheat, and corn—which provide greater price transparency and liquidity for trading and hedging."

Also consider getting help from firms experienced at scaling up businesses. New Cannabis Ventures' Alan Brochstein—also known as the 420 Investor—says that at this point, it can be helpful to generate additional "awareness and connect with potential investors, B2B customers, strategic partners, and the media."

One final option to consider is diversification. Mull over building additional businesses around your original one. "For example, in Washington state, dispensaries are not allowed to sell T-shirts, water, food, glass, anything like that," Blues Traveler's Brendan Hill says. "So my partner and I decided to take over a little space next door to our dispensary, Paper & Leaf, this year, and build out an ancillary products shop where we sell coffee, sandwiches, snacks, vaporizers for nicotine . . . This is a regular business that attracts our dispensary customers, generating extra money while allowing us to make tax deductions."

"Expansion takes a lot of work; it will take lawyers and a team of people," Cannabis Culture's Jodie Emery cautions.

Going Multistate

A point will arrive when you will want to go multistate with your company. However, before crossing state lines, make sure that every aspect of your business is working perfectly within your initial state. Especially if you will license your product in other states, make sure quality remains consistent.

One of the best bets for companies looking to expand into multiple states is looking at states that have just recently legalized cannabis. These states will see a lot of new businesses pop up and uncountable underserved needs around them. "Every state that opens up offers opportunities for a set of businesses that already exist in other states to launch in that state," Scott Greiper notes.

"When a market legalizes the cultivation of cannabis, it creates a set of new opportunities related to the geographical constraints that exist," New Frontier Data's vice president of industry analytics John Kagia adds, pointing to the illegality of interstate commerce that U.S. cannabis producers, processors, and manufacturers face and the fact that this trait makes the industry hyperlocal, almost like no other.

Remember that "the rules of the state where you started your business do not apply when you enter a new state," MJIC's CEO Sturges Karban says. "In addition, commercial dynamics will be different in every state, brands will be different, (and) the fundamentals in general will be different."

To conclude, Karban shares this example: imagine you wanted to build a hotel in China. You wouldn't be able to just go there and do it successfully; you'd need a local partner. "Even though it may sound crazy, in some ways, the difference between two states like California and Colorado, transactionally, culturally, legally, and commercially, is as wide apart as the U.S. is to China," he says. Partnering up with a local could help ease your path in this new market.

So by this point, you'll probably have a business going and will be acquainted with the cannabis industry, its perks, and its quirks. It's time to grow.

To get ready to expand and even go multistate, you will need to:

▶ Get additional, expert help.
▶ Assign clear roles to everyone in your company.
▶ Differentiate your business and create barriers for new entrants.
▶ Create a strong customer service framework.

▶ Start giving back to the community, the industry, and the patients.

▶ Make sure your quality remains consistent through diverse locations and states.

▶ Learn about the laws in other states.

▶ Get local partners to help you with expansion.

▶ Pay every tax, and always remain compliant!

You might think that once you have a business up and running, the challenges will disappear. However, more often than not, new ones will arise—as will the need for specialists to deal with certain aspects of your expanding business, such as operational efficiencies, workers' compensation and incentives, etc. So get ready because things are about to get hectic. This is the time to get help, get acquired, or get lost.

CHAPTER

11

Get
Fired
Up

I f there is one central conclusion you could draw from

every interview conducted for this book, it's this: starting

a business is hard. Really, really hard. If it weren't, then

everyone would do it.

So be prepared to feel out of your depth; to need help

and not know where to get it; to face problems you had

never anticipated; to work day in and day out.

Keeping a business from failing is already tough, but making it really successful is "a major challenge that not many people accomplish," Cannabis Culture's Jodie Emery says. (Emery herself owned several well-known companies by the time she was 32.) Nonetheless, if you've gotten this far in the book, you should be ready to overcome all challenges.

Don't be scared; be ready. Don't worry; do what needs to be done. Don't shy away from trials; embrace them. The road to financial success is paved with tribulations. Fortunately, you are now equipped to face them.

Admittedly, starting a cannabis business is even more difficult than starting a regular business. You will face social stigma, complex and often conflicting regulations, high risks, difficulty in accessing capital, hurdles in your growth path, and many other issues.

Even though cannabis is being legalized all over the world, "there is still a lot of stigma to get over, (and) communities still frowning on it," Emery says. "If you decide to open a cannabis-related business, some people will call you a drug user, or a druggie, or say that you are doing something dangerous or harmful to society or believe you are destroying people's brains and health. There are all sorts of hysteria and fear still out there."

But the rewards will be worth the effort and heartache. Every time a patient, a kid, a parent, or a veteran thanks you for your work, you'll feel that warmth in your heart that few other industries can offer.

It bears repeating: be prepared to face all the risks—legal and reputational—involved in being part of the cannabis industry. But don't be afraid to be a disruptor either; it's often those who don't shy away from risk who are the most successful. Finally, make sure you love what you do; it's probably the best way to achieve your goals.

"Getting into the cannabis industry will be very discouraging and very difficult in many ways, but the more people that we see take a shot at it and get out there, the better it will become," Emery says. "To get into this industry, you will need a little bit of bravery and a little bit of courage because there are going to be normal business challenges and some unfair extra challenges."

"Entrepreneurs in the [cannabis] space have to take on not only the typical risks of being an entrepreneur but [also] the added complexity and burden of working among a myriad of regulatory rules at the local, state, and federal level," EVIO Labs' co-founder and COO Lori Glauser says. "Entrepreneurs in the cannabis industry must deal with challenges ranging from highly stringent security protocols, limited access to banking, complex and costly tax rules, neighbors who don't want you doing business in their community, and competitive application processes to attain cannabis licenses. Regardless of the state-level acceptance, cannabis is still illegal according to the feds, so we work exceedingly hard to ensure that we work in accordance with all state and local rules so there is a lower risk that the feds will want to interfere.

"Our legal status makes doing things as simple as getting business insurance, credit card processing, or even a lease for a copier very challenging," she adds. "Traditional vendors often won't accept the business risk of working with a cannabis-related company."

Another factor to consider is the value and importance of the cannabis movement. People partaking in cannabis like to see that you and your business are involved in giving back to the community. But if you do, you will be received with open arms and become a part of something much larger than yourself, your business, or even your community. You'll be part of a movement for human well-being and for people everywhere.

Luckily, the cannabis industry is one of the friendliest out there. Many people will be willing to help you and support you as much as they can. But "never depend on others for your success," Daniel Cheine warns. Even in an industry as collaborative as the cannabis industry, "no one is going to throw you a pile of money or a bag full of blueprints on how to achieve success," he says. "It all will depend on hard work, dedication, discipline, and constantly trying to be the better version of yourself. Day in, day out."

In the end, it's about trusting your gut. "When you fully believe in your vision, go all in on it," the Cronos Group's Michael Gorenstein says. The best way to instill trust in others is to show you trust yourself.

On the bright side, we are at a pivotal moment for the cannabis industry. "Most in the industry expect that cannabis will eventually be legalized federally," Lori Glauser says. "So those of us who are successful today will be very well-positioned when this industry becomes like just another crop or just another pharmaceutical or nutraceutical or an alternative to alcohol."

"There is a wealth of educational and financial opportunities in this space," Gia Morón, founder and CEO of GVM Communications, adds. "This industry is filled with multifaceted challenges, [so] it requires professionals who are equipped to address issues, promote brands, and build relationships with media."

"We anticipate that large brands will come in and there will be a lot of consolidation of businesses in the future. So the entrepreneur who is preparing now for that eventuality could reap benefits, either by participating with the industry alongside the alcohol, tobacco, and pharmaceutical companies or by preparing to get acquired by them," Glauser concludes.

But there's something important to keep in mind about success, CannaSOS' Oleg Cheine says: "The higher you go, the thinner the air and the more difficult it is to keep the same friendly relationships with your team. Why? Because each person will begin to count the money in your wallet and will think that they are getting paid less than everyone else. If you can properly motivate your team, no one is going to look in your wallet and everyone will support you in hard times.

"The success of any business depends on many factors, but the main factor is this: what team you will have and how loyal your team will be will have a huge impact on the success of your company," he adds.

As your company begins to thrive, make sure you don't change as a person, the Cronos Group's Michael Gorenstein cautions. "There are things that made you successful when you started the company," he says. "If you start to change personally, that will affect things, people will notice in the company, and the faith that they put in you will get lost."

Our final piece of advice: stay grounded. You don't want to lose the things that made you successful or drive away the people who accompanied you on your way to the top.

Cannabis entrepreneurs said again and again during the interviews conducted for this book that it's still early—the industry is only in the second inning of the game, so to speak. "There is a lot of innovation for small startups in the space because the industry is still forming," MJIC's Sturges Karban says.

But beware: "People get paralysis by all of these new ventures and ideas, products, and segments that don't exist and maybe sometimes shouldn't even exist. So focusing is really important," Cura Cannabis Solutions' Cameron Forni warns. "Really focusing on what you are good at, focusing on your company, and not getting sidetracked by every shiny thing that's in front of you is key."

Get into the cannabis industry while you can. The train won't wait. Whether you hold a BA from a state university, a graduate degree from MIT, or only made it through eighth grade, the time is now. It's the green rush! Hop on!

Welcome, everyone.

Cannabis Business Resources

They say you can never be rich enough or thin enough. While that's arguable, we firmly believe you can never have enough resources. Therefore, we're giving you a wealth of sources to check into, check out, and harness for your own personal information blitz.

These sources are tidbits—ideas to get you started on your research. They are by no means the only sources out there, and they should not be taken as the ultimate answer. We have done our research, but businesses do tend to move, change, fold, and expand. As we have repeatedly stressed, do your homework. Get out there and start investigating!

General Resources

- ▶ An interactive map of cannabis and hemp legality by state: http://norml.org/laws
- ▶ A directory of attorneys servicing the cannabis industry: http://lawyers.norml.org
- ▶ A tutorial on business plan writing from the SBA: www.sba.gov/business-guide/plan/write-your-business-plan-template
- ▶ A directory of accounting firms servicing marijuana businesses: www.ganjapreneur.com/marijuana-accounting-firms
- ▶ Another directory of accounting firms servicing marijuana businesses: https://industrydirectory.mjbizdaily.com/accounting
- ▶ An up-to-date, state-by-state list of qualifying conditions for medical marijuana use: www.leafly.com/news/health/qualifying-conditions-for-medical-marijuana-by-state
- ▶ Banks, credit unions, and payment-processing firms servicing the cannabis industry: https://industrydirectory.mjbizdaily.com/banking-point-of-sale

Data Analytics Companies

- ▶ The Arcview Group generates in-depth market research: https://arcviewgroup.com
- ▶ Baker Technologies focuses mostly on point-of-sales and customer data: www.trybaker.com
- ▶ BDS Analytics also offers point-of-sales data, in addition to consumer research and industry intelligence: www.bdsanalytics.com
- ▶ Cannabis Benchmarks has one of the most complete data sets on the wholesale market: www.cannabisbenchmarks.com
- ▶ Consumer Research Around Cannabis creates cross-referenced local consumer preferences data: www.consumerresearcharoundcannabis.com
- ▶ Eaze shares sales data and consumer preferences information: www.eaze.com
- ▶ GreenWave Advisors releases reports on the state of the industry, lab testing, retail sales, and the coexistence of legalized medical and recreational marijuana markets: www.greenwaveadvisors.com
- ▶ Headset focuses on market data, business intelligence, and retailer-direct data: http://headset.io
- ▶ Marijuana Business Daily publishes reports on financial benchmarks and business facts, as well as a licenses directory: https://mjbizdaily.com
- ▶ New Frontier Data dives deep into the state of legal cannabis markets across the globe and in numerous U.S. states, as well as sales projections, diversity reports,

investor studies, tax collection and potential estimates, and industrywide trends: https://newfrontierdata.com

▶ Viridian Capital Advisors tracks stock performance, capital raises, and M&A activity in the public and private sectors: www.viridianca.com

Compliance Software

▶ CannaRegs: http://cannaregs.com
▶ Complia: https://mycomplia.com
▶ iComply: www.icomplycannabis.com
▶ MJ Freeway: https://mjfreeway.com
▶ Simplifya: www.simplifya.com
▶ WebJoint: www.webjoint.com

Family Office Experts

▶ Cavendish Global: http://cavendishglobal.com
▶ The Family Office Club: http://familyoffices.com
▶ Family Office Networks: https://familyofficenetworks.com
▶ SCN Corporate Connect: www.smallcapnation.com

Venture Capital Funds, Angel Investing Organizations, and Private Equity Firms

▶ Ackrell Capital: www.ackrell.com
▶ AngelList: https://angel.co
▶ The Arcview Group: https://arcviewgroup.com
▶ Benchmark Capital: www.benchmark.com
▶ Canna Angels: https://cannaangelsllc.com
▶ Casa Verde Capital: www.casaverdecapital.com
▶ Floris Funds: http://florisfunds.com
▶ Founders Fund: http://foundersfund.com
▶ Green Growth Investments: www.greengrowthinvestments.com
▶ Halley Venture Partners: www.halleyvp.com
▶ MedMen: https://medmen.com
▶ Merida Capital Partners: www.meridacap.com

- Navy Capital: www.navycapital.com
- Phyto Partners: www.phytopartners.com
- Poseidon Asset Management: https://poseidonassetmanagement.com
- Privateer Holdings: www.privateerholdings.com
- Salveo Capital: www.salveocapital.com
- Tress Capital: www.tresscapital.com
- Tuatara Capital: www.tuataracapital.com
- Viridian Capital Advisors: www.viridianca.com

Industry-Specific Holding Companies

- AmeriCann Inc. (OTC:ACAN): http://americann.co
- Cronos Group (CVE:MJN) (OTC:PRMCF) (FRA:7CI): http://thecronosgroup.com
- Diego Pellicer Worldwide (OTC:DPWW): www.diego-pellicer.com
- Doyen Elements: http://doyenelementsus.com
- General Cannabis (OTC:CANN): www.generalcann.com
- Golden Leaf Holdings (CSE:GLH) (OTC:GLDFF): http://goldenleafholdings.com
- iAnthus Capital Holdings (CNSX:IAN) (OTC:ITHUF) (FRA:2IA): www.ianthus-capital.com
- Innovative Industrial Properties Inc. (NYSE:IIPR): www.innovativeindustrialproperties.com
- MassRoots (OTC:MSRT): www.massroots.com/investors
- MJIC Inc.: www.mjic.com

Cannabis Business Accelerators and Incubators

- CanopyBoulder: www.canopyboulder.com/home
- Canopy San Diego: http://canopysd.com
- Freedom Leaf: www.freedomleaf.com
- Gateway: www.gtwy.co

Traditional Accelerators Accepting Cannabis Businesses

- 500 Startups: https://500.co
- The Launch Incubator: www.launchincubator.co
- Y Combinator: www.ycombinator.com

Cannabis Crowdfunding Platforms

▶ CannaFundr: www.cannafundr.com

▶ CrowdfundX: www.crowdfundx.io

▶ 420fundme: http://420fundme.com

▶ Fundanna: https://fundanna.com

Recommended Reads

Abel, E.L. *Marihuana: The First Twelve Thousand Years.* Springer, 1980.

Backes, Michael. *Cannabis Pharmacy: The Practical Guide to Medical Marijuana.* Black Dog & Leventhal, 2014.

Barcott, Bruce. *Weed the People: The Future of Legal Marijuana in America.* Time Books, 2015.

Blaszczak-Boxe, Agata. "Marijuana's History: How One Plant Spread Through the World." *Live Science* (October 17, 2014). www.livescience.com/48337-marijuana-history-how-cannabis-travelled-world.html.

Clarke, Robert C., and Mark D. Merlin. *Cannabis: Evolution and Ethnobotany.* University of California Press, 2016.

DeAngelo, Steve. *The Cannabis Manifesto: A New Paradigm for Wellness.* North Atlantic Books, 2015.

Drug Policy Alliance. *A Brief History of the Drug War.* www.drugpolicy.org/issues/brief-history-drug-war.

Hasse, Javier. "Why Hemp Could Be the Future of Plastics." Benzinga (May 5, 2017). www.benzinga.com/markets/emerging-markets/17/05/9405826/why-hemp-could-be-the-future-of-plastics.

Hasse, Javier. "Why Industrial Hemp Could Prove a Larger Economic Driver Than Marijuana." *High Times* (September 11, 2017). https://hightimes.com/business/why-industrial-hemp-could-prove-a-larger-economic-driver-than-marijuana/.

"Hemp 101: The Ecology of Hemp." Recreator (April 20, 2017). https://recreator.org/blogs/hemp-101/hemp101the-ecology-of-hemp.

Herer, Jack. *The Emperor Wears No Clothes: Hemp and the Marijuana Conspiracy.* AH HA Publishing, 2010.

Holland, Julie. *The Pot Book: A Complete Guide to Cannabis.* Park Street Press, 2010.

Jones, Nick. *Spliffs: A Celebration of Cannabis Culture.* Chrysalis Impact, 2003.

Kalant, Harold. "Medicinal Use of Cannabis: History and Current Status." *Pain Research and Management* 6, no. 2 (Summer 2001): 80-94.

Martino, Joe. "Hemp vs Cotton: The Ultimate Showdown." Collective Evolution (July 17, 2013). www.collective-evolution.com/2013/07/17/hemp-vs-cotton-the-ultimate-showdown/.

Mikuriya, T. H. "Marijuana in Medicine: Past, Present and Future." *California Medicine* 110, no. 1 (January 1969): 34.

NORML. *Marijuana Law Reform Timeline.* http://norml.org/shop/item/marijuana-law-reform-timeline.

O'Connell, Kit. "How Hemp Can Heal Our Soil & Why It Matters to Consumers." Ministry of Hemp (April 27, 2017). https://ministryofhemp.com/blog/hemp-soil-remediation/.

PBS. *Busted—America's War on Marijuana.* www.pbs.org/wgbh/pages/frontline/shows/dope/etc/cron.html.

Rätsch, Christian. *Marijuana Medicine: A World Tour of the Healing and Visionary Powers of Cannabis.* Healing Arts Press, 2001,

Rosenthal, Ed. *Beyond Buds: Marijuana Extracts—Hash, Vaping, Dabbing, Edibles and Medicines.* Quick American Archives, 2014.

Russo, E. B. "History of Cannabis and Its Preparations in Saga, Science, and Sobriquet." *Chemistry & Biodiversity* 4, no. 8 (August 2007): 1614-1648.

Walton, R. P. *Marihuana, America's New Drug Problem: A Sociologic Question with Its Basic Explanation Dependent on Biologic and Medical Principles.* JB Lippincott Company, 1938.

Public Relations Firms

- ► Bridge Strategic Communications: www.bridgestrategic.com
- ► The Cannabis Story Lab: http://thecannabisstorylab.com
- ► Cannabrand: http://cannabrand.co
- ► 5WPublic Relations: www.5wpr.com
- ► GVM Communications: www.gvmcommsinc.com

- Higher Ground: www.highergroundagency.com
- KCSA Cannabis: www.kcsa-cannabis.com
- Kip Morrison & Associates: www.kipmorrison.com
- McGrath/Power: www.mcgrathpower.com
- NisonCo: http://nisonco.com
- North 6th Agency: www.n6a.com
- Potnt Agency: www.potnt.com
- Powerplant Strategies: http://powerplantstrategies.com
- Precise Cannabis: www.precisecannabis.com
- Proven Media: http://provenmediaservices.com
- The Rosen Group: http://rosengrouppr.com
- Rosie Mattio PR: www.rosiemattiopr.com
- Salar Media Group: www.salarmediagroup.com
- Verdant Communications: www.verdantcomm.com
- Zoe Wilder: https://zoewilder.com

Cannabis-Focused Customer Engagement Firms

- Baker Technologies (www.trybaker.com/) uses an online platform to generate foot raffic, repeat visits, and loyalty among its customers.
- The Daily Leaf (http://dailyleafdeals.com) offers deals and discounts on its site to direct new customers your way.
- Green Marimba (www.greenmarimba.com) offers a similar SMS marketing service.
- SpringBig (www.springbig.com) uses SMS to get new customers through your doors.

People Interviewed for this Book

- BDS Analytics managing director and principal analyst, and Arcview Market Research editor in chief Tom Adams
- SCN Corporate Connect founder and CEO Hugh Austin
- Avicanna CEO Aras Azadian
- Green Light Law Group's cannabis attorney Bradley Blommer
- The Cannabis Story Lab co-founder Karen Blondell
- Electrum Partners president Leslie Bocskor
- True Leaf Medicine International CEO Darcy Bomford

- Former *Forbes* cannabis writer and Green Market Report CEO Debra Borchardt
- 420 Investor and New Cannabis Ventures founder Alan Brochstein
- Proven Media vice president Neko Catanzaro
- *High Times* director of digital media Emily Cegielski
- CannaSOS co-founder Daniel Cheine
- CannaSOS co-founder Oleg Cheine
- SCN Corporate Connect managing director Bryan Crane
- Canna Advisors co-founder and principal Diane Stratford Czarkowski
- Canna Advisors co-founder and principal Jay Czarkowski
- Famed cannabis activist and businessman Steve DeAngelo
- New Frontier Data founder and CEO Giadha Aguirre de Carcer
- Cannabis legalization activist and marketing expert Jerome W. Dewald
- Compassionate Certification Centers co-founder and CEO Dr. Bryan Doner
- CanPay CEO Dustin Eide
- Cannabis Culture co-owner and famed cannabis activist Jodie Emery
- iAnthus Capital Management managing director Hadley Ford
- Cura Cannabis Solutions co-founder and president Cameron Forni
- New Frontier Data executive vice president of communications & government affairs Gretchen Gailey
- Iron Protection Group co-founder and CEO Hunter Garth
- EVIO Labs co-founder and COO Lori Glauser
- The Cronos Group CEO Michael Gorenstein
- HERB founder and CEO Matt Gray
- Viridian Capital Advisors founder and president Scott Greiper
- Hamilton Investment Partners managing partner Douglas A.P. Hamilton
- *Shark Tank* original host and founder of As Seen on TV Kevin Harrington
- Blue Cord Farms CEO Robert Head
- California's Bureau of Cannabis Control cannabis policy analyst Amelia Hicks
- Blues Traveler drummer and cannabis entrepreneur Brendan Hill
- Jeff The 420 Chef
- New Frontier Data executive vice president of industry analytics John Kagia
- MJIC CEO Sturges Karban
- GreenWave Advisors founder Matt Karnes
- High Pressure Zone co-founder JJ Kaye
- Documentary director and podcast host Mehka King
- Gateway accelerator co-founder and managing partner Ben Larson

- ▶ Canna Ventures founder and principal Eric Layland
- ▶ CrowdfundX director of marketing Aaron Mendez
- ▶ The Cannabis Marketing Lab founder and CEO Celeste Miranda
- ▶ Wick & Mortar founder and CEO Jared Mirsky
- ▶ Former NFL player and cannabis investor Joe Montana
- ▶ GVM Communications founder and CEO Gia Morón
- ▶ Floris Funds president Skip Motsenbocker
- ▶ IGC CEO Ram Mukunda
- ▶ Cannabis brands designer Felipe Nosiglia
- ▶ Iron Protection Group co-founder Caleb Patton
- ▶ Professor at Yale University's School of Medicine Dr. Godfrey Pearlson
- ▶ Viridian Capital Advisors vice president Harrison Phillips
- ▶ Purple Haze Properties CEO and president Andrew Pitsicalis
- ▶ Former Mexican President Vicente Fox Quesada
- ▶ International law expert Zameer Qureshi
- ▶ Civilized founder and publisher Derek Riedle
- ▶ New Leaf Data Services CEO Jonathan Rubin
- ▶ Salar Media Group CEO Cynthia Salarizadeh
- ▶ Phyto Partners founder and managing partner Larry Schnurmacher
- ▶ Leafly co-founder and Headset co-founder and CEO Cy Scott
- ▶ Benzinga managing editor Jason Shubnell
- ▶ The Cannabis Story Lab co-founder and principal John Sidline
- ▶ Green Flower Media founder and CEO Max Simon
- ▶ Benzinga head of newsdesk Brent Slava
- ▶ The Green Solution co-founder and CEO Kyle Speidell
- ▶ Consumer Research Around Cannabis vice president Jeffrey Stein
- ▶ Canna Advisors director of client operations Tyler Stratford
- ▶ CanopyBoulder co-founder and managing director Micah Tapman
- ▶ 7 Point Law cannabis lawyer Anne Van Leynseele
- ▶ Former NFL player and cannabis entrepreneur Marvin Washington
- ▶ *Forbes* and *New York Times* cannabis writer Julie Weed
- ▶ Jane West CEO and Women Grow co-founder Jane West
- ▶ MSNBC's *The Pot Barons of Colorado* co-star and serial cannabis entrepreneur Andy Williams
- ▶ WeedFeed owner and cannabis-focused community manager Christine Young
- ▶ Paragon co-founder and CanopyBoulder graduate Sam Zartoshty

We want to thank every one of the people mentioned above. This book would not have been possible without your help, guidance, input, and continued support.

Glossary

Angel investor: an investor who provides money for a business venture in exchange for equity or convertible debt. These investors tend to provide more flexible and often more favorable lending terms for the startups they fund.

Business Accelerator or Incubator: accelerators or incubators take in nascent businesses and train their founders for material success. Beyond the mentoring, accelerators often make small investments in the businesses they take in, in exchange for sizable ownership.

Cannabidiol: a compound that is one of the primary constituents of cannabis.

Cannabis: a type of flowering plant with at least three known species: Cannabis sativa, Cannabis indica, and Cannabis ruderalis. Cannabis indica and cannabis sativa are used to produce cannabis "buds," normally known as marijuana, weed, or pot.

CBD: a chemical compound found in marijuana, industrial hemp, and hops plants. It is believed that CBD has no psychoactive effects. In fact, it is often said that CBD actually reduces the psychoactive sensation generated by THC. As such, it is frequently used to treat children and adults suffering from epilepsy and other grave ailments and brain disorders.

Cole Memo: A memorandum drafted by United States Deputy Attorney General James M. Cole intended to provide legal protection for caregivers ("individuals providing care to individuals with cancer or other serious illnesses, not commercial operations cultivating, selling, or distributing marijuana"). The Cole Memo reiterated the importance of prosecuting drug traffickers (rather than state-legal producers and retailers) established in the Ogden Memo, although it did not protect legal cultivators from federal prosecution.

Cole Memo 2.0: an updated version of the Cole Memo, which was recently rescinded. This memo exhorted federal authorities to stay out of states' issues, letting local law enforcement agencies and regulators decide the fate of their legal cannabis businesses, incentivizing a "hands-off" approach.

Crowdfunding: a mechanism used to raise capital for a business from regular, non-accredited investors.

Dabs: a type of cannabis concentrate with a sticky, honey-like texture, which can be consumed via "flash" vaporization in which users place the product on a very hot surface and inhale what comes out, normally using a pipe of some kind.

Dispensary: colloquial denomination used to refer to licensed cannabis and cannabis-products retailers.

Edibles: colloquial denomination for any kind of cannabis-infused food or drinks.

Family Office: a private wealth management firm similar to a hedge fund but serving just one or a few very wealthy families and high net worth individuals.

Hemp: also known as industrial hemp, a variety of the cannabis sativa species with very low levels of THC. Hemp is usually grown with the purpose of being processed and turned into other products like fibers, papers, fabrics, fuels, oils, etc.

ICOs: a fundraising mechanism in which companies issue a virtual token similar to—and often based on—Bitcoin or Ethereum and sell them to the public under the promise that they will surge in value.

Impact (or Socially Responsible) Investments: investments focused on business opportunities that can not only generate strong capital returns but that can also have a positive impact on the society as a whole—or at least in the community in which they will operate.

Mood Board: a visual presentation including images and text, conceived to reflect the "essence" or style envisioned for a brand during the design phase.

Ogden Memo: a memorandum released on October 19, 2009, conceived as a guide for U.S. Attorneys on "the exercise of investigative and prosecutorial discretion" with the intention of steering the use of investigative and prosecutorial resources from "individuals whose actions are in clear and unambiguous compliance with existing state laws providing for the medical use of marijuana" toward "significant traffickers of illegal drugs, including marijuana, and the disruption of illegal drug manufacturing and trafficking networks."

Seed Investor: an investor who provides the initial money for a business venture.

Series A Round: a capital raise conducted after the initial seed round. Proceeds are usually used to help move the company into normal operations and scale up.

Sublingual Tincture: a liquid cannabis extract usually based on alcohol.

THC: the so-called psychoactive ingredient in weed. THC is often responsible for getting cannabis users "high" or "stoned."

THCa: a non-psychoactive chemical present in cannabis plants which, when dried, loses its A (or acid) component, creating THC.

Valuation: how much a company is worth to the market. A company's valuation will be often determined by how much of the company's equity is needed to give out in exchange for the money received, rather than by an actual calculation of a company's potential value or net worth.

Vaporizing: a way of consuming cannabis flowers or oils without combustion or smoke in which consumers can get the active ingredients of cannabis in the form of vapor.

Index